Humphry Did It!

Janice N. Chapman

ISBN 978-1-955156-68-4 (paperback)
ISBN 978-1-955156-69-1 (digital)

Copyright © 2021 by Janice N. Chapman

All rights reserved. No part of this publication may be reproduced, distributed, or transmitted in any form or by any means, including photocopying, recording, or other electronic or mechanical methods without the prior written permission of the publisher. For permission requests, solicit the publisher via the address below.

Rushmore Press LLC
1 800 460 9188
www.rushmorepress.com

Printed in the United States of America

Other Works by Janice N. Chapman

Novels

Destiny's Call
Pieces of a Cowgirl's Life
They Called Him RJ
Trail Number Four
Visitors of the Unknown

Poetry

Writin' the Range
Love, Lies, and Heartaches
Poems With No Place To Go

Short Story Collections

Legacy of Short Stories and Essays
Priceless Pages from Amazing People

Introduction

There are among us folks who are completely faultless—to hear them tell it, that is. They need someone to place the blame on other than themselves.

And that poor little guy named Humphry became their fall guy for their blame and their own shortcomings. In his early life, he was blamed for things his older brother did and was given a daily ration of "Humphry did it!"

He was later adopted by James Cotton and raised on the Slant T ranch near Miami, Oklahoma, where James Cotton worked. One of the other cowboys taught him to play a guitar, and in later years, Humphry became a singing star. By then the accusations of "Humphry did it!" were spoken with pride and praise.

1

Who is Humphry? Well, he was chubby, happy-go-lucky, round-faced little boy with sandy-blond hair and dark brown eyes and a ready smile. He was five years old, and as you can imagine, he was a charming little imp standing just over four feet tall.

The first time I saw Humphry, he was leaning against a fence post down by the corral, watching the four young fillies play. His eyes twinkled, and his face wore a beautiful friendly smile. And right away I liked him.

Some youngsters, I don't particular like because of their attitudes and disrespect for their elders and kinfolk. But Humphry? Who couldn't like Humphry? His charm was contagious!

Humphry was like a fresh breath of fresh air—the more I was around him, the more I wanted to be.

"Hi, mister. Did you come to watch the babies too?" he asked me as he turned his head to look my way.

I dismounted and walked over to where the kid stood and told him, "Yeah, I guess I did."

He held out a chubby little hand and said, "I'm Humphry! I'm glad you came. What's your name?"

"James," I told him, shaking his chubby little hand, then crossing my arms on the top rail of the corral. "Do these babies have names?"

"Sure! That one over there is Smoky." He pointed to a mouse-colored filly with white stockings on her back legs. "And that one over there with the white streak down its face is Bets. The yellow one right here is Jigger." He moved his little arm moved to his left. "And that brown-and-white one is Splash."

"Which one do you like best?" I asked him.

"I like 'em all!" he said, his excitement in his voice catching me off guard.

"Well, all right then," I commented.

I didn't know any other little boys his age who liked horses enough to spend hours at a time watching them and enjoying their antics.

"Humphry! You get in here this minute!" There was sarcasm in the woman's voice. "What have I told you about talking with strangers?"

Humphry laughed at the woman who no doubt was his mother. That seemed to anger her more.

But Humphry paid no attention to it and gleefully told her, "He's not a stranger. He's my friend. He's James, and he's my friend."

"Humphry you get in this house! *Now*!" she told him, turning to me. "Who are you and what do you want here?"

"Ma'am, I stopped here hoping I could water my horse and fill my canteen," I told her.

"The pump's over there," she snapped, pointing across the yard.

She turned and flounced hastily into the house and slammed the door behind her.

I walked my horse over to the pump and caught him a bucket of water with the bucket setting next to it. All the while, I wondered what sort of punishment that cute little boy had been given once he went into the house. I heard the woman's voice still yelling at him.

I had just put the bucket back where I'd found it when a teenage boy stumbled out into the yard, raising his voice to lament, "But, Mama, I didn't do it. Humphry did it!"

Well, I didn't know what Humphry did or was accused of having done, but if Humphry did it, it must have been before I came along and stopped at the corral.

I filled my canteen, walked my horse to the house, and then knocked on the door.

Anger still flared in the woman's face and voice when she opened the door and demanded, "What do you want?"

"I wanted to thank you, ma'am, for letting me water my horse and fill my canteen," I told her, trying to keep my voice civil. "And to ask if you know anyone around here that might be hiring."

She studied me for some long moments before she answered with some measure of control in her voice, "I could use some help around here, but I can't hire anyone because I can't pay wages. I need what little I have to feed the youngins. So no, I don't know anyone hirin' right now."

"I see," I said.

I started to turn to go, but then I thought of that little boy Humphry.

I turned back to her and offered, "How about if I stay long enough to get your pens and fences back in shape for you? I could sleep in the barn and maybe hunt down a deer for your family to eat."

Again, she studied me for long moments before she asked, "Why would you want to do that?"

"Well, for one thing, ma'am, it looks to me like you've fell on hard times, and I'd like to help if you'll let me. Besides I like your little boy," I told her.

She was silent for a long time, seeming to be staring out across her land. Humphry came out of the house to stand beside her, still smiling that beautiful smile of his. And the older boy sidled up beside her on the other side. This teenager was almost to her shoulders. He had brown hair and eyes and at the moment was wearing a smirk on his shallow face. He wasn't chubby like Humphry, but he wasn't skinny either. There were quite a few years between him and little Humphry. I figured the woman had lost some babies in between these two boys, but I didn't pry.

Most folks didn't like to talk about that sort of thing anyway.

It was Humphry who broke the silence.

"You aren't leaving us, are you, James?" Humphry asked in a cheerful voice.

"I guess so, Humphry. Your mom doesn't seem to want me to stay and help fix up the place," I told him.

"Well, me and Wayne want you to stay," Humphry told me.

Wayne I supposed was the older boy.

"Why do you want him to stay? He's just some stranger, and we don't even know him!" Wayne glared at Humphry as he spat those words at him.

I had to admit, Wayne had a point.

Humphry was still smiling, and he told Wayne, "He's my friend. And his name is James. And he ain't no stranger."

"Humphry, that will have to be left up to your mother," I told him. "Right now I need to go back to that town I saw at a distance a few miles back and pick up a few things."

"Don't take too long, James. I want you to come back!" Humphry said, looking up at me with innocent wide eyes.

"We'll see," I told him, not wanting to commit to anything, smiling at him.

"You better 'cause we have to go to bed when the sun goes down! And that doesn't leave you much time!" Humphry said, applying that beautiful smile of his.

"Humphry, stop that! Leave the man alone!" his mother scolded.

Humphry laughed and told her, "He's not a man! He's James. And he's my friend."

"He can't be your friend, Humphry. You barely met him," his brother Wayne stated irritably.

I backed my horse a few feet so he wouldn't hit any of them, and then I turned and rode out of their yard with little Humphry's voice ringing in my ears, "Don't be gone too long, James!"

The town was small, with only a few houses, a stable, a grocery store, a bar, and an eating joint. I left my horse at the stable so he could eat some grain and some hay. The owner charged me a dollar for the feed and fifty cents for the grain and thirty cents an hour for stable rent. I thought it was a little high, but Gunner needed the grain and hay. So I left him there while I went to the grocery store. I bought what I needed for the trail for myself, and then I asked him if he had some peppermint sticks.

"How many do you want?" he asked.

"All of what you have on hand," I told him.

I figured the boys would enjoy them, especially that brown-eyed little imp with that heart-winning smile. The clerk found a paper bag and dumped the jar of peppermint sticks into it.

"Will there be anything else?" he wanted to know.

I thought a minute, and then I asked him to fix a burlap bag with food stuff for Humphry's mother. He raised his eye brows questioningly.

"That would be Mrs. Hargrove. I didn't know she had money to buy that many groceries, and I can't give her any more credit," he told me.

"Fill the bag with staples and foodstuff. I'll pay for it, and I'll pay her bill too," I answered. "Give her dried beans and . . . whatever women buy to cook for their families."

He found a burlap bag, shook the dust from it, and filled it for me. The bag came to fifty-three dollars, and her bill was thirty dollars and twelve cents. I paid him and thanked him. I started to leave, but he stopped me and asked how I knew Mrs. Hargrove.

"I don't. I stopped by there to ask for water for my horse and to fill my canteen. Then I offered to stay on and help fix the place up. But she said she can't pay anyone to help her because she needs what little she has to feed the boys with. So I'm going to take these groceries out to her on my way back through," I replied.

"That's good of you, mister. Bye the way, I'm Jeffery Bowers."

"James Cotton," I told him and shook hands with him.

"Be glad you're passin' through. That woman's got a mouth that could scald the hide off a hog. That oldest boy is lazy as the day is long. And that little one . . . well, everybody likes him. But if something gets out of place, whether or not he did it, the older boy is quick to blame it on the little one, and Mrs. Hargrove lets him get by with it," Jeffery Bowers told me.

"Thanks for the warning," I told him. "I need to go get my horse and be on my way."

"Come back any time," Bowers told me as I left his store for the livery.

Gunner was ready to go. I tied the burlap bag onto the saddle and brought my bed roll with me as I mounted him. The livery man charged me twenty cents for his rent. I paid the man and rode once more to the Hargrove place.

The sun was threatening to go down when I rode into the yard. This time I rode up to the house, took the burlap bag from my saddle, retied my bedroll, and knocked on the door.

The woman opened the door a few inches and, seeing me, loaded her voice with sarcasm when she asked, "What do you want?"

"I want to know where to set this bag of groceries," I told her.

She looked at me as if I was the most ridiculous person in the world. And I have to admit I felt ridiculous just standing there holding the groceries I knew she needed. After what seemed like an eternity, she told me to follow her into the kitchen where she had me lay the bag on the table.

She looked at me with angry eyes and stated hatefully, "I can't pay you for these."

"I didn't ask you to," I told her. "I paid your bill at the store, so you don't have a bill there now."

"I didn't ask you to do that or to buy us groceries either!" she stated.

"No you didn't," I agreed. "I paid your bill off to help you out. And I bought the groceries for you so that you and the boys don't have to go hungry for a while. I did it because I wanted to, and I did not expect you to pay me for anything, not even for the bag of peppermints I bought for the boys."

2

Mrs. Hargrove gave me a hard distrusting look before she opened the burlap bag. Right there on top was that paper bag filled with the peppermint sticks I had bought for the boys. Neither she nor I had heard the boys creep up behind us and didn't know they were there until Wayne spoke up.

"Those are mine!" he declared.

"No," I told him. "I bought those for both of you boys, not just for you."

"May we eat one now?" Humphry's sweet little voice asked.

She looked at him, her expression softening some, and told him, "Just one. I don't want you to ruin your supper."

She handed each boy one peppermint stick, folded the bag, and then set it on a shelf at the top of her cabinet. After doing that, she came back to the table and took the rest of the groceries out of the burlap bag. She sorted them and put them where she wanted them, leaving out what she wanted to fix them for supper.

Finally she looked at me and told me, "Thank you, James. I guess you can find a place in the barn to sleep and put your horse there too. I think there's room. If not, then turn the mares out into the corral with the foals."

I thanked her and left the house and led Gunner to the barn. I stopped just inside of it and lit a lantern that hung on a nail a couple feet to the right of the door. The inside of the barn looked as bad as the outside. I didn't know how long the mares had been penned up inside their stalls, so I led each of them outside and turned them into the corral. They were glad to be out and to be able to exercise in the corral. One mare stopped at the water tank and drank her fill before joining the other three in trotting around the corral's perimeter. Watching her, I decided I had better fill the tank again. It meant several trips to the pump, but at least the mares and foals had water.

I left Gunner ground reined while I cleaned out the stalls—all six of them. It took a while.

All of them looked as if it had been a long time since they had been cleaned last. By the time I finished, the barn had aired out some, and I elected to leave the door open overnight so it could air out more. When I had laid out my bedroll in the far back stable, I decided to turn Gunner into the corral with the mares and foals for the night. He didn't need to spend the night in a foul-smelling barn stall. The mares welcomed his company, and the foals showed off for him in their playful manner.

Sometime during the night, the wind began blowing—not hard but hard enough that it aired the barn out for me. By morning, it had calmed down to a slight breeze. I was up at my usual time, which was about daybreak. There were no lights in the house, so I filled the water tank in the corral again.

Leaning against the corral, I pondered what to do today and where to start and what was the more important thing that needed doing. As I watched the horses mill around in the corral, I decided the top of the list would be to ride that fence to what seemed to indicate a pasture. There was plenty of grass right there near the corral, which told me there should be plenty of grass over the entire acreage. I had not noticed any tools of any kind anywhere in the barn. There weren't any fencing supplies either, for that matter.

I caught Gunner and saddled him. Then he and I began our tour of that pasture fence. The farther I rode, the more disgusted I became. Their fence looked like a war zone. I found broken wires, tree limbs across it in places, and downed wires in other places, not to mention broken posts throughout the tour Gunner and I were taking. It would take at least a couple of days of work to get together again. But I was right about one thing—grass was abundant all the way through it. I let Gunner graze a few minutes before I rode back to the barn.

When we rode up to the barn, Humphry was there to greet us. His hair was still trussed up from sleeping, but his heartwarming little smile was very much in place.

"Hi, James! I thought you had left again," he blurted out.

"No," I told him. "Me and Gunner just took a trip out in the pasture to check the fence."

"Oh! Well, Mama has breakfast ready! Come on in and eat!" he invited.

I pulled the saddle off Gunner and turned him into the corral and followed this jolly little imp into the house.

His mother did indeed have breakfast of bacon, eggs, and fresh biscuits ready. She had fresh coffee too. And I found she was not only a good cook, but she could make a good pot of coffee too.

"Where's Wayne?" I asked.

"He's around here somewhere," Mrs. Hargrove replied nonchalantly.

"I could use his help today fixing that fence. I rode it this morning. It will take a couple of days to get it back to where it should be," I told her.

"He gets up in the mornings and leaves the house. I don't know where he takes off to," she answered me, sounding much like she didn't care where he was as long as he wasn't home.

"Do you have a saw or axe around here someplace?" I asked. "There are some tree limbs across parts of the fence that I need to get moved. And if you have any wire, I could wire the fence up in places. And there are a few broken posts here and there."

"I didn't asked you to fix my fences," she reminded me sarcastically.

"Ma'am, if you don't let those mares of yours out to graze soon, you're going to lose them. Horses can't live on a few handfuls of grain once a day."

I don't know if she cared a whit about the horses. I was sure her oldest son did not care for anything, including the horses. And little Humphry wasn't old enough to take care of them the way they should be taken care of.

"Why don't you just leave and leave us alone?" she snapped.

"I'm going to leave. But I'm going to town and get what I need to fix that fence so those horses of yours can eat and exercise," I stated flatly, trying to be as sarcastic to her as she was to me.

Once outside, little Humphry told me, "When you get back, James, I'll help you with the fence."

I smiled at him and said, "Thanks, pard."

I rode to town to the livery stable. The owner watched me ride up. I asked him if he had any small wagons I could buy or rent—anything I could haul a few supplies in.

"I may have one in the back, but if I do, we may need to fix it before you can use it," he told me.

"Let's have a look at it," I said.

In the back of his barn, he had an old wagon. It looked like it had been built for just exactly what I needed it for. The wood was gray from the weather, but it looked to be in fairly good shape. It needed cleaning up and the axles greased, but it would work. I asked him how much he wanted for it. He told me since we need to clean it up, he would let me have it for five dollars. I asked him if he had a horse and harness for pulling it. I didn't think Gunner needed to be pulling a wagon.

"I have a mare. She's gettin' on in age, but she'll pull a wagon," he commented.

He helped me clean and grease the wagon, then he brought out the harness and the mare and hitched her to the wagon.

"How much for the horse and harness?" I asked him.

"That depends on what you want to do with them," he told me.

"I need to get some fencing supplies to fix the pasture fence on Mrs. Hargrove's pasture. She has some mares and foals that she's been cooping up in her barn. They need to be turned out to grass soon or she's going to lose them," I told him.

"Want some help?" he offered.

I couldn't have been more surprised, and I assured him I would certainly appreciate the help.

"By the way, I'm James Cotton," I said by way of introduction.

"Dick Sweney. Let's go down to the store and get those supplies you need, and I'll help you get that fence in working order," he responded.

I let Dick Sweney drive the wagon down to the store while I followed on Gunner. It was a short trip, but it gave me time to see how well the little wagon pulled. At the local store, we loaded it with the fencing supplies we figured we needed, including posthole diggers and fencing pliers. I paid the merchant. I tied Gunner at the back of the wagon as there was room for both me and Dick Sweney on the seat, and we headed back to Mrs. Hargrove's place.

When we arrived, I had Dick pull up to the gate, going into the corral from the yard. The horses came to it to introduce themselves to the new mare.

Mrs. Hargrove brought her wrath with her, demanding, "Just what do you think you're doing!"

"We're going to fix the fence so these horses can be let out there to graze and exercise," I told her.

"You can leave my fences alone! Turn that wagon around and get off of my place!" she spat at us.

"We will, just as soon as we get through with the fence, ma'am," I said, trying to hold back the anger I felt.

It was hard for me to believe the woman was so callous that she would let her stock starve to death rather than let us fix her fence for her, especially since we were doing it for free for the sake of the horses. It wasn't costing her one little copper penny. I should have thought she would have been grateful for the help, seeing as to how her fourteen-year-old son was lazy and shiftless and well versed in telling his mother "Humphry did it!" on everything and anything he didn't want to own up to.

I walked over to the gate that led into the pasture and let the mares and foals out, knowing the mares would quickly find a place to graze; the foals, too, after showing off a few minutes, would begin to eat their fill of the grass.

Sweney pulled the wagon through that gate, and I closed it after him. Mrs. Hargrove stared after us, seething in the knowledge that we had ignored her outrage. When I turned around to go back to the wagon, Humphry appeared, seemingly out of nowhere.

"Can I go with you, James?" he asked, his smile lighting his face with expectancy.

"Of course you can, Humphry," I told him.

I handed him up to Dick Sweney who scooted over a few inches so Humphry could sit next to him. And we headed toward the first repair spot in the fence. We reset the post there and moved on to the next place. It didn't take long to finally come to the first place where the tree limbs were across the fence.

While Sweney and I set about cutting and removing the limbs from the fence, I untied Gunner and let him graze. He had more than earned his right to eat, I thought. When we were through with that problem and put the tools back in the wagon, Humphry picked up Gunner's reins and followed the wagon, with Gunner following him.

Gunner had never been around children until I came to the Hargrove place. In a way, I was surprised the stallion took up so readily with Humphry. Then again, with Humphry's carefree manner, his beautiful smile, and being young—I could somewhat understand it. By the time we reached the next bunch of tree limbs across the pasture fence, I knew Gunner would look after Humphry. When Sweney and I were through with mending the fence, I asked Humphry if he would like to ride Gunner. You never heard such excitement as when Humphry said yes.

"Before we get in sight of the house, Humphry, I'll have to take you off of him so you don't get in trouble with your mom," I told him.

"I know that, James," Humphry agreed, his excitement exceeding cloud nine.

I tightened the cinch and lifted Humphry on to the saddle and handed him the reins. Then I told Gunner to follow the wagon. He rubbed my shoulder with his face, letting me know he would follow my instruction—he would have anyway with Humphry on his back. I don't really know who enjoyed the walk back the most, Humphry or Gunner.

A half mile from the house, I took Humphry down from his throne on Gunner and lifted him to Sweney who again made room for him on the wagon seat.

3

I left the gate to the pasture open so the horses could come in to the corral for water. I had Sweney pull the wagon over to the door of the barn and closed the gate to the yard. I ground reined Gunner and helped Humphry down. He helped me and Sweney unload the tools and store them in the last stall at the back of the barn.

"Thanks, Humphry," I told him.

He smiled, and his eyes lit up. I had a notion this little five-year-old had not been told "thank you" very often in his young life, and compliments were probably just as rare.

We had just finished putting the tools up when Mrs. Hargrove appeared at the wagon, hands on her hips and a tongue of wrath that would have embarrassed sarcasm.

"I told you to get off my place and leave us alone!" she informed me. "Now get! And don't let me find you on my place again!"

"Mrs. Hargrove, he has only been trying to help you," Dick Sweney told her. "I don't know why you are so mad about someone helping you."

"I didn't ask you. And you can get off my place too!" she snarled at him.

Sweney looked at me, and I raised an eyebrow and gave him a slight nod. He walked around the wagon to where Mrs. Hargrove stood with her hands still on her hips.

"You know . . . I never had a daughter," he said. "But if I had I'd sure want to know she was a good woman. One who would take care of her children. One who was not too proud to accept help out of kindness from people who care about her."

She actually removed her hands from her hips and folded her arms across her breasts.

"I know it's hard to raise youngins alone, ma'am," Sweney continued talking. "And it's doubly hard when you don't have anything and nothing to look forward to except for more hard times. But it gets harder when you have to watch your livestock starve and then your young ones starve and maybe even yourself, all because of stubborn pride."

I swear I saw tears in Dick Sweney's eyes, and I thought that perhaps he spoke from past experience. Then he did something totally unexpected. He walked over to Mrs. Hargrove and put an arm around her shoulders.

"I know a lot of people take advantage of a person when they are down and out, and no doubt some have taken advantage of you as well," Sweney continued in a fatherly tone. "But not everybody is that way. Some folks try to help out of kindness and the goodness of their hearts because they are good Christian people. And if you've read the Bible at all or listened to preaching during your life, then you know God tells us to do unto others as we would have them do unto us."

He paused for a few moments to let that sink in.

"James here is trying to help you, ma'am," he added. "He came here peacefully, and he is trying to leave your place in better shape than it was when he rode in yesterday. Not many people would do that just to help you out. He's not doing it for money. He is doing it to help you and the boys and to be a friend."

Dick Sweney took his arm from around Mrs. Hargrove and stepped away from her. She looked at him, and it seemed some of her wrath melted away. Maybe she had never had anyone talk to her the way Sweney had.

"Maybe I've been wrong," she said in a halfway decent tone. "I have never had any friends to speak of. Most people do try to take advantage of me, especially since my husband died. I've always had to pay for anything that was done for me. So I don't trust folks too easily."

"That's understandable," I told her. "But I didn't come here to harm you or your boys."

Little Humphry, who had gone over to keep Gunner company, came to his mother and asked her in his innocent five-year-old voice, "Mom, does that mean you'll let my friend James stay?"

She unfolded her arms and hugged Humphry to her and whispered hoarsely, "I guess so, Humphry. If he wants to stay after all I've said to him."

I knew it took a lot for her to say that, and I think her son felt that too. Most of the time, he was an easygoing little boy with a smile that took my heart away. But right now, he seemed much older than his few years, and he was sincere with his question.

At his mother's answer, his little face brightened, but again he said sincerely, "He wants to stay, Mama, and I want him to stay. I like James, and you will too when you get to know him better. He may have to leave in a few days, but couldn't you try to like him while he's here?"

I came around the wagon to stand beside Humphry and his mother.

I spoke to her, saying, "It's okay, ma'am, if you don't like me. I had no right to insist on staying against your wish. I just wanted to help get your place back in shape, if you'll let me. I would feel better knowing I had done something to help you and the boys before I leave. It may come down to you having to sell it later on, and it will bring more if it is fixed up. But if you really want me to leave, I can leave in the next few minutes."

"No you can't, James!" Humphry told me. "I'll help you fix whatever else needs fixin'!"

Humphry was near tears, and the bright that had lightened his face a few minutes ago left it. He was looking up at me with a face of longing—almost begging—with his expression and his eyes for me to stay on with them.

His mother took her cue from Humphry. That was the first time she talked in an almost pleasant tone.

"James, will you stay a few more days with us? And can you forgive me for the things I've yelled at you these past two days?"

I knelt by Humphry and took him into my arms. He clung to me. His young body was trembling. I held him close. He needed that moment. I looked up at his mom and told her yes, I could forgive her and yes, I would stay a few more days.

Moments later, Humphry turned loose of me, and one of his enchanted smiles took its place on his face.

"Thanks, James. I'm glad you're going to stay a few more days. I didn't want you to leave us."

"I need to get Mr. Sweney back to town. Is it all right if Humphry comes with us and rides back with me on the wagon?" I asked Mrs. Hargrove.

"Yes, he can go with you. But isn't that Mr. Sweney's wagon? Seems like he could drive himself back to town," she said.

I smiled and told her, "No. The wagon belongs to you, and so does Rosebud as soon as I pay him for her."

She looked at me in surprise and uttered, "You didn't—"

"Oh yes I did," I interrupted. "After I leave, you are going to need a way to go get groceries and whatever else you need. I didn't see a wagon anywhere around here. You can't walk to town, which I presume you have been having to do. Sweney wasn't using this wagon. You also don't have a horse trained to pull a wagon. Rosebud has a little age on her, but she will last a few more years. And she is trained to pull the wagon."

"I'll have supper ready when you two get back." she told me.

"Thank you."

I lifted Humphry up to Dick Sweney and climbed up beside him. Rosebud had rested and was now ready to get back to town. I let her have her head, and she settled in to a mile-eating trot.

"Sweney, thanks for your little pep talk with Humphry's mom. I don't know who all has done her wrong. But I know she has lost a husband and some babies along the way. She's alone against the world, miles from anywhere, so I guess she had a right to be distrustful."

"Distrustful, yes," Sweney stated. "But not raw-bone mean and hateful the way she turned on you, James. You must have reminded her of someone in her past. Or it could be that after some of the ordeals she has gone through she was afraid to let herself get too close to you."

"I expect that Humphry here gets more than a fair ration of her temper too. I didn't notice her getting after the older boy the way she does this little fellow," I replied.

"Wayne don't never stay home much," Humphry told us. "He leaves the house in the mornings and sometimes doesn't come home until real late. But Mama doesn't seem to mind him doing that."

"Doesn't she worry about him?" Sweney asked.

"No. She just tells me she knows he will be back after a while. She doesn't make him help with the chores, which is mostly to water the foals, and I don't mind doing that. I like to watch them play. Sometimes I catch little birds or frogs or rabbits. But I have to let them go because they have their own homes to go to," he said.

"Doesn't your mom have Wayne bring in the firewood and help with the dishes and such?" I asked.

"No, James. I bring in the firewood. I usually have to do the dishes and sweep the floors. And I make Wayne's and my bed too," he answered.

Sweney shook his head and looked over at me. I thought I knew what he was thinking. Like me, I figured he didn't like the idea of Wayne taking off every day and his mom not caring that he spent all day, and sometimes part of the night, away from the house. Neither he nor I liked the idea of a five-year-old having to do the things Wayne should have been helping with. Wayne was old enough to look after the mares and to keep those stalls in the barn cleaned out. Humphry was too young yet for those tasks.

I stopped at the livery, and Sweney got down from the wagon.

"Dick, how much do I owe you for the mare and the rigging?" I asked him.

"You already paid me for the wagon. I guess I forgot to tell you the mare goes with it," he replied.

"Thanks for helping with the fence today," I said.

"I'll come out tomorrow and we'll see what else needs done," he told me.

Humphry ask if he could drive us home. When I got Rosebud straightened out toward his house, I let him have the reins. In that moment, he was ten feet tall. His excitement lit up his face, and his smile took its place. Even in the looming dusk, I could see how proud he was.

He did a good job of driving the wagon. I'm sure Rosebud would resent me for saying that out loud. Together they got the wagon home and next to the corral. I got down then helped Humphry down.

"You did a good job of getting us home," I told the boy.

In his young life, he needed all the praise he could get.

"I'll put Gunner and Rosebud in with the rest of the horses, and then I'll be in," I told him as I started unhitching Rosebud.

I put her in the corral. Then I unsaddled Gunner and led them both on through the corral to the pasture, removed their bridles, and turned them loose. Before I went in to the house, I put the wagon harness and my gear in the barn in the stall I had slept in the night before.

Mrs. Hargrove had a nice supper on the table. I stepped to the washstand and washed my hands and face and dried them on the towel lying beside the washbasin before I sat down at the table.

"Looks good," I told her.

She gave a slight smile before she sat down opposite me at the table.

Wayne sat sullenly on her right side; and Humphry, beaming like a light bulb, sat on her left.

We had eaten supper pretty much in silence. As we finished, Mrs. Hargrove asked her sons if they would like another peppermint stick. Humphry was quick to answer yes, while Wayne didn't say anything. Their mother got up and went to the cabinet where she had put them the day before. The peppermints were gone, sack and all.

"What happened to that bag of candy?" Mrs. Hargrove asked with anger in her voice.

Her oldest son was quick to say, "Humphry took it!"

"Humphry couldn't have took it. He hasn't been here all day," she told him.

"Well, I didn't do it! It had to have been Humphry!" Wayne shouted at her.

For a moment, I thought she was going to slap him. I felt like it myself.

"Why don't you go look under his pillow on his bed?" I suggested, at which point Wayne's face and neck began to turn pink.

Moments later, his mother emerged from the boys' bedroom with a half-empty sack of the peppermint sticks.

"Young man, how did these get under your pillow?" she demanded of Wayne.

"I don't know. Humphry musta put 'em there," he said hatefully, his blushing belying his falsehood.

Wayne did not know Humphry had been with me all day since breakfast and had gone with me to take Sweney back to town. Wayne had gotten home just before we did.

"You are a liar, Wayne Hargrove!" his mother stated angrily.

"I am not! Humphry did it!" he spat at his mom.

"And *when* did Humphry do it?" she demanded.

"He did it after lunch!" Wayne insisted.

"Would you mind telling me *how* Humphry done it when he wasn't even here?" she prompted.

"I don't know, but I didn't do it! I wasn't here either!" Wayne retorted sarcastically.

"You just said it was done after lunch. Humphry wasn't here for lunch," his mother reminded him.

I had forgotten that Humphry had missed lunch, and so had Sweney and me.

Wayne got up from the chair he had been sitting on at the table, halfway turned to face his mother, and yelled out, "Why do you always take up for Humphry? You don't ever take up for me!"

Mrs. Hargrove's eyes flashed anger, and her words again took on that scathing tone.

"Young man, how dare you speak to me like that! You sit down in that chair, and don't you move until I tell you to!" She pointed to the chair Wayne had just moments ago vacated.

His face was crimson red now, and I thought I saw tears well up in his eyes. But for the life of me, I couldn't find it in me to feel the least bit sorry for him. He sat back down, and Mrs. Hargrove took her seat also and sat facing him.

"I'm going to tell you this and one time only," her voice had a deadly quiet tone that dared her son to speak out to defy her. She seemed completely unaware of Humphry and me. "You are fourteen. You are nine years older than Humphry. You get up every morning and run off to God knows where, leaving your younger brother to do the chores as best he can. He's not old enough or strong enough to take care of the mares. But he does try. You, on the other hand, are lazy and shiftless, and you don't do anything but whine. But that is fixing to change, young man. You either will stay at home and help out around here or I will put you in an orphanage. And you had better be listening because I am through with your crap. Is that understood?"

Tears had spilled out of Wayne's eyes and were now running down his face. He nodded to his mom and whispered, "Yes, ma'am."

"I know you took the candy, Wayne, because Humphry left this morning to help James and Mr. Sweney fix the fence around the pasture. He wasn't here. They didn't get back until late this afternoon. So he wasn't here for lunch either. After that, he went with James and Mr. Sweney to take Mr. Sweney back to town. He and James got back just before we sat down to eat supper. James and Humphry missed lunch all together," she informed him. "I know what goes on around here, whether or not you want to believe it. So don't you ever lie to me again!"

Wayne made his way around another "Yes, ma'am."

I didn't know what to say, so I didn't say anything. I was proud that Mrs. Hargrove had finally decided to be a mother and to try to discipline that oldest boy of hers. And I hoped he would listen to her and straighten up. But deep down inside, I had serious doubts that he would ever really straighten up. He might make a few gestures along to appease his mother. But I didn't think it was in him to actually straighten out and be the son he needed to be. Feeling sorry for himself was deeply ingrained, as was his selfishness.

I knew little Humphry was in for some hard years after I left. His only salvation was that either Wayne got old enough to leave home and did so or that he himself could leave home when he was old enough. He was only five now, and I hoped through the years he could endure his brother without it warping his own personality.

"Mrs. Hargrove, would it be all right for Humphry to have a peppermint stick? He did work pretty hard today, and he really does deserve one," I said.

She didn't say anything. She continued to stare at her oldest son. But she had heard me, and she reached into the sack and handed Humphry a peppermint stick.

He took it and told her, "Thank you, Mama."

Then he came around to me and leaned against me. I put an arm around him while he ate his candy. He made it hard for me to think about leaving.

Mrs. Hargrove glared at her oldest son for several more minutes before telling him, "Go to your room, Wayne. You are not getting any more candy. You've already eaten half a bag of it. The rest is for Humphry."

I stood up and took my arm from around the younger boy. I told her I needed to be going.

Humphry's face fell, and he asked, "Do you really have to go, James? Couldn't you stay a few more days?"

"No, Humphry. I really need to go. I have some business elsewhere I need to give some attention to. Maybe when I get that taken care of, I can stop back by," I answered him.

I was surprised that Mrs. Hargrove stood up and came around to us. I was fully expecting a round of scalding words from her.

Instead, she told me, "Thank you for everything you have done for us, James. And I apologize for the way I have treated you ever since you rode in. I hope you can stop back by when you are through with your business."

You could have bowled me over with a feather.

I walked outside and went to the corral and called Gunner. He came at a leisurely walk.

But that was okay. He and I had a long ride ahead, and he would need all his strength along the way. He stood still while I saddled him. I walked him through the gate into the yard.

Humphry had come outside and now stood at the edge of the porch. I walked Gunner over to him and gave him a hug. Gunner snickered to him softly and reached his muzzle over to give the youngster a kiss on his cheek. Humphry put both arms around the stallion's face and gave the horse a hug.

"You be a good boy till we get back, son," I told him.

He nodded, too choked up to speak, and watched us ride out of the yard.

"You hurry up and get back here, James!" Humphry shouted after me.

I felt sorry for Humphry. He had lived a hard life, especially if his mother had been as sarcastic before I had come along as she was when I came. But still, I had done all I could do for them in the few days I had lingered. The only thing I could say "Humphry did it!" about was this guilty feeling that came over me shortly after Gunner carried me away from their yard.

I can't remember any other kid affecting me so emotionally inside as Humphry did. His easygoing personality, his beautiful smile, his sparkling eyes, and his cheerful tone—they combined to grab at a person's heart. I wasn't sure about his mother's heart. In fact, I wasn't sure she had one. But Humphry's ways had grabbed my heart and held on tight. And even if I didn't get back this way, I would never forget that chubby, round-faced little boy that even my stallion loved. And Gunner wasn't taken in by too many people, young or old. He had been a herd stallion at the time we brought him in. He wasn't the most trusting horse I had ever dealt with. And I took several extra days to train him and gain his trust while breaking him.

But for some reason, he came to love Humphry in those few short days. Maybe because he was young. It was a two-way match.

5

It was almost dark, but it had cooled down and felt good to me. I didn't often ride in the dark, but I needed to put some miles behind me. Gunner was rested and had grazed for several hours on the pasture. He was ready to go and fell into an easy lope that put miles and time behind us. Now and again, he slowed to a trot for a mile or so before stretching into a lope again. I let him have his head.

It was almost midnight before I pulled him down and hobbled him on a grassy spot a few feet where I chose to put my bedroll and sleep until morning.

Sleep didn't come easy. My mind kept going over the past few days and Mrs. Hargrove's scathing tones when she spoke. Maybe I couldn't blame her. After all, I was a stranger, and she had been taken advantage of by others. Maybe she did have a right to be distrustful and mean. I wondered if she actually would crack down on Wayne or if she would let him go on with his irresponsible ways. She wasn't doing him any favors if she let him keep on with doing the things he was doing. It wasn't fair to his little brother to have to hear "Humphry did it!" day in and day out, especially coming from Wayne.

I was glad I was able to implant at least a couple of happy memories into Humphry's young mind, letting him ride Gunner and letting him drive the wagon home from town. Those were memories his young five-year-old mind would cling to forever.

I finally drifted off to sleep and woke when the warm muzzle of my stallion brushed my right cheek.

"Morning, Gunner. Thanks for waking me," I said.

Gunner snickered softly.

HUMPHRY DID IT!

I got up and stretched, then rolled up my bedroll and saddled Gunner. Today would be another long day in the saddle.

Gunner stepped out in that easy mile-eating lope of his. Birds sang in the early morning.

Some of them swooped down to check us out as we passed their territories. Others sang and made the morning pleasant for both me and my horse.

"Gunner ol' boy, let me know if you happen to see a watering spot somewheres," I told the stallion.

He twitched his ears and snickered as if to tell me okay. The prairie we were crossing had few trees even. It was mostly straight and flat. The grass was green enough and so were the cacti that were flowered out here and there. And maybe if I didn't think about it too much, the heat from the sun wouldn't seem so hot.

By my calculations, I was still three long days away from Guymon—shadeless hot days away from Guymon. It was late in the afternoon when Gunner moved his ears forward and raised his head to look at the land ahead of us. I couldn't see what he was looking toward, but animals sense things long before us humans do. In less than a quarter of a mile, he began to quicken his pace, almost running full out. I let him run. When he fell back into a walk, I could see what he had been anxious to get to. There in the middle of nowhere was a natural spring, flowing pure, sweet water into a small pool that overflowed across the ground. It wasn't deep, but it was surely welcome.

I let Gunner drink his fill, I drank a good bit myself, and then I filled my canteen. After that, I wet my bandana and wiped my face. I rinsed it out and washed Gunner's mouth and nose and rinsed it out again before tying it back around my neck. If felt good on my neck. Its cool moisture ran a chill down my back, but it was a welcome chill after riding so far in the day's heat.

I took a piece of beef jerky from my saddlebag and sat down to eat it. I let Gunner graze for a while. The grass around that little spring was green, and Gunner seemed to enjoy it. Maybe it was sweet grass. He ate like there was no tomorrow. But finally, I climbed aboard the saddle and we ventured onward.

I had ridden several miles when we heard a growling sound. Gunner stopped dead still, his ears forward. It was only a second before the growling was followed by the biggest badger I had ever seen in my life. I backed Gunner until the badger stopped coming at us. Then I turned him north for a ways, and we went around that badger's territory. Badgers are the only thing I know that have claws as long as or longer than a bear's. I am not afraid of them, but I do have a healthy respect for them.

The shadows were long in the late evening when we found a small stand of trees that welcomed us to share the night with them. I unsaddled Gunner and found some broken pieces of wood to build a fire with. When it blazed to where I wanted it, I made a small pot of coffee, careful not to use more water than I needed from the canteen. Again, I snacked on a piece of beef jerky. As I chewed on it, I began thinking about Humphry. I wondered how much trouble the little guy had gotten into for telling me to hurry back, and how much his brother Wayne had continued to pick on him and bully him. Had Mrs. Hargrove kept her word about not putting up with any more of Wayne's crap, or had that been for my ears only? Had he resumed his laziness the next morning or had his mother really set her foot down? I hoped she had.

When I had first stopped in at their place, Mrs. Hargrove hadn't seemed to mind that her oldest son stayed away from home all day with her not knowing where he was or what he was doing. It had taken the words from Dick Sweney to bring her back to reality.

I had never married, so I had never had a son to raise. But if I had, I would have wanted him to be like little Humphry—jolly, friendly, and easygoing, with a love for life that knew no strangers. Humphry is one of those people who never meets a stranger. He recognizes people as friends. He wouldn't know what a stranger is. I think even criminals and outlaws would love Humphry.

We were still a couple of days away from Guymon, Gunner and I. I was anxious to get there. It would be new to Gunner. I had bought him from my boss, Grant Rayes, who had bought him from a ranch near east Miami, Oklahoma, not too far from his own Slash T ranch a couple of years ago where he had ran free as a herd stallion. It had taken a lot of my hard-earned savings, but Gunner had proven himself worth it. He wasn't registered, but he his lineage went back to Three Bars. I never can remember his dam's lineage, but he stands sixteen hands high. And I love everything about him, right down to his blue-roan, dark gray color. He was a green broke three-year-old when I bought him from Mr. Rayes. It wasn't hard to get him gentled down and put a bit of training on him. We kind of grew on each other, I guess.

* * * * *

Sleep covered me up finally. And again in the morning, Gunner woke me. He was better than an alarm clock. And I am thankful he is. We had miles to cover. Miles we needed to put behind us before the sun scalded us with its burning heat.

"After today, Gunner, we will only have one more day to travel before we will be home," I told him as I tightened the cinches.

Gunner turned his head and offered a low snicker as if to ask me, "Where's home?"

As I mounted, I told him, "You have never been to where I grew up, Gunner. But I think you'll like it there. 'Course it could have changed some in the years I have been gone. But it will still be good to be back again."

Gunner's answer was that easy mile-eating lope of his.

Midday found us in an area of low rolling hills. Now and then a coyote watched us ride by. And the light breeze blew dried tumbleweeds at us. A couple of them just missed hitting the stallion. But he seemed to pay them no mind. That afternoon, we came upon a windmill that was busy pumping water into a large cow tank. I let Gunner drink his fill, and then I filled my canteen. We were about to leave when a rifle spoke a warning shot.

I looked around and, not seeing anyone, I called out, "I just needed to water my horse and fill my canteen. I'll be glad to pay you for the water."

I saw him then. He must have been watching from the other side of that little knoll yonder. Anyway, that's the way he came from. I waited on him to walk on down to us. He wasn't too tall. He was thin, but he looked like a sure-enough Oklahoma cowboy.

When he came up, I said to him, "I'm James Cotton. My folks live on over near Guymon. I just needed to water Gunner and fill my canteen before going on."

"Well, in this part of the country, a body has to be real careful, Mr. Cotton. I'm Dale Simmons. Are you by any chance Andy and Loraine Cotton's son?" he asked me.

"Most folks just call me James. And yes, those are my parents," I answered him.

He smiled then and offered his hand for a handshake. "They're mighty nice folks. I've known them for a few years now."

"I've been gone for several years," I told Mr. Simmons. "I was coming home to visit for a few days and check on them and see how they are. It will be good to be home again."

"Let me get my horse and I'll ride a ways with you," Simmons offered. "As a matter of fact, why don't you come on home with me and get a good meal and a bed and spend the night? I expect the horse can use some rest too and a bait of grain."

I took him up on it. A meal sounded a whole lot better than beef jerky right now. And for certain, Gunner could use the grain.

The evening meal Mrs. Simmons served was the best I had eaten in some time. I thought Mrs. Hargrove was a good cook, but her cooking didn't even compare to that of Mrs. Simmons. Her roast duck was cooked to perfection, tender and mouthwatering. Her mashed potatoes were just as good as my mom's. The biscuits were light and fluffy. And the green beans were seasoned to excellence as well.

"Eat hearty," she told me. "We have plenty of everything."

I had seconds of everything. That's how hungry I was.

"Dale tells me you are Andy and Loraine's boy. We have known them for a long time. I know they'll be glad to see you. We don't get to see them often, but we like them and consider them friends of ours," she stated.

"I should be there in another day. I'll be glad to see them too. I've been working down in southeast Oklahoma near Miami on a ranch called the Slant T. It's owned by Grant Rayes. I saved up enough to buy my horse and gear. Then I talked to Mr. Rayes and told him I wanted to visit my folks. He told me to go ahead and that my job will be waiting for me when I get back," I explained to Mrs. Simmons.

I helped her clear the table, and then she showed me to an empty bedroom where she said I could get a good night's sleep. I thanked her and went out and brought my gear in and placed it at the foot of the bed.

Tired as I was, it was a long time before I drifted off to sleep . . . only to be woken later hearing a loud voice yelling "Humphry did it!" It startled me awake.

I sat up on the side of the bed, looking around. There was no one in the room. Looking out the window, I saw nothing outside that should have disturbed my sleep. What had happened to Humphry? Was he in trouble again? And who did that voice I heard belong to? It wasn't his mothers. And it wasn't Wayne's. But it was a voice. One completely unknown to me. I couldn't go back to sleep for thinking about Humphry.

At length, I heard Mrs. Simmons in the kitchen preparing breakfast. The aroma of freshly made coffee ran stride for stride down the hall with the smell of frying ham slices. After a few minutes, I went ahead and got out of bed, spread the bed like it had been the night before, and ambled toward the kitchen. I was just a couple steps ahead of Mr. Simmons.

Mrs. Simmons poured both of us a cup of coffee and asked me, "Do you take cream or sugar, James?"

"No, ma'am, but thank you for offering," I said.

"We talked it over last night, James, and we decided if it is all right with you, we'd like to take you on over to your folks' place, and that way we could visit with them a while ourselves," Mr. Simmons spoke now. "I can hitch the stock trailer to the pickup and haul your horse for you. It will get you home quicker. And I'm sure your horse would appreciate getting there sooner without having to carry you all day again."

"I appreciate that, Mr. Simmons," I told him, "I'm sure you won't get any argument out of Gunner."

"Okay then, let's eat, and we will be on our way," he commented.

I think my taste buds jumped for joy when I bit into the first bite of ham. Never had I eaten ham so tasty. And my sunny-side-up eggs were like two yellow eyes surrounded by white eyeballs daring me to eat them with the ham. I did. I enjoyed every bite.

I helped Mr. Simmons with hitching the stock trailer to the pickup before retrieving my saddle from the bedroom I had slept in. I set it in the back of the pickup, then went to get Gunner.

Gunner greeted me with his usual morning snicker. I petted him a moment, then put the bridle on. As I led him toward the pickup, I told him, "You get to ride today, Gunner. And we will be home in a couple of hours or so."

Gunner stopped at the back of the trailer. He looked it over, looked at me, and then loaded like a champion. I stepped in and took the bridle off him. As I stepped out of the trailer, Mr. Simmons closed the gate behind the stallion.

I laid the bridle in the bed of the pickup with the saddle. Then I climbed into the passenger side of the vehicle, which put Mrs. Simmons in between her husband and me.

"That sure is a pretty horse you have," Mrs. Simmons said. "I don't think I've ever seen one that color of gray before."

I told her thank you. I didn't know what else to say.

Sitting next to the door on the passenger's side of the pickup, I could look out across the endless miles of flat land that were accented the closer we got to Guymon with low rolling hills.

It was as if I could see forever as we traveled. I was glad Gunner and I didn't have to spend today with me riding on him as we crossed this land. The closer we got to Guymon, the more I could see civilization had moved in while I had been gone. Even the stockyard at the old sale barn had grown bigger. It was more than twice the size I remembered it when I left years ago.

The town itself had spread out to the west of the sale barn, and I almost didn't recognize the turn when Mr. Simmons turned right on to the dirt road leading to my where my parents lived. It was several more miles to their house, and the dirt road was rough. No one had taken time to grade it since the last rain had come through the area.

I suppose it was my imagination, but the place, when we reached it, seemed smaller now than it had those years ago when I left it. Maybe it was because I was so much younger then that it had seemed so much bigger.

Mom stepped outside to meet Mr. and Mrs. Simmons. They were as happy to see her as she was them. They exchanged hugs, and then Dale asked where Dad was. Mom told him Dad had gone to the store for her and he'd be back soon.

"Come see what we brought home to you," Dale invited Mom.

She followed him to the trailer where I was unloading Gunner.

"James!" she exclaimed, tears of happiness flooding her eyes as she engulfed me in her motherly hug. "I'm so glad you're home! My goodness, let me look at you!"

I smiled and hugged her back.

"This is Gunner, Mother," I told her as I introduced her to my stallion.

Gunner rubbed his head against my shoulder and muttered a soft snicker as if to ask who this female person was.

"Gunner this is Mother," I told him. "You'll love her too."

"He's pretty, James. I don't think I have ever seen a horse quite that color before," she told me.

"Where can I put him, Mom?" I asked her.

"Just put him in the corral, James, and come on in the house and have some tea with us," she said.

With that she turned to Mrs. Simmons and they walked arm in arm into the house.

Gunner followed me closely as I led him to the corral and turned him into it. I watched him trot around it while I made sure there was water in the stock tank. Satisfied there was plenty of water in the tank, I went into the barn in search of grain for Gunner. There was only a sack not quite half full of oats sitting inside one of the stalls. I didn't see anything to put grain in, so I gathered a few scoops of oats into the crown of my hat and took it to Gunner and poured it onto the ground for him to eat. Then I wiped out the crown of my hat with my bandana to get the dust from the oats out of it and put it back on top of my head.

Funny, but that gesture of putting my hat back on brought thoughts of Humphry to mind.

I could hear his mother telling him she had told him not to talk to strangers and his comeback, "He's not a stranger—he's James, and he's my friend!" I shook my head to clear it and walked back to the house. Mother would love Humphry and his easygoing ways and that beautiful, heart-grabbing smile of his. Maybe after a while, I could tell her and Dad about him and how much of a sweet child he is and how he lived almost daily hearing "Humphry did it!"

I went back to the house, washed my hands, and poured myself a glass of tea. Mom always left the sugar shaker setting out so that those of us liking sweeter tea could help ourselves to putting extra sugar into our tea. I joined the grown-ups in the living room and listened to their conversations as I sipped my glass of tea.

HUMPHRY DID IT!

After the years I had spent in the bunkhouse at the Slant T, being indoors with my parents and Mr. and Mrs. Simmons seemed strange. They were discussing cattle and ranching strategies. Dale Simmons had finished the well where I had watered Gunner and caught a canteen full of water for myself. He mentioned fencing that piece of range with the new barbed wire. Dad also had land he wanted to fence with it. And after discussing its overall effectiveness, they decided they would help each other with the fencing. And with me helping, they could get the fences up sooner and could then drive their prospective cattle herds onto the pastures.

Their conversation turned to the new hybrid wheat that had recently been announced in association with the farming industry. This was a new winter wheat that had originated in Canada or so the rumors had it. The more they talked about it, the more it became a good idea. They weren't farmers, but who said ranchers couldn't raise wheat too? It would mean buying plows, drills, combines, and trucks to haul their harvest to the elevators. But if the farmers could do it, the ranchers could do it, they reasoned. They already had tractors and haying equipment, so if they caught a year that the wheat didn't produce, well, they could bale it and use it for winter feed. Dad had cut and baled prairie grass for years, so baling wheat would not be anything new for him. Besides, the wheat could be used for pasture during the months the winter grass didn't grow. They would just have to pay attention and pull the cows when they needed to. But it would save them on the amount of hay they would have to have every winter. After harvest, they could again turn the cattle into the fields to clean up the wheat stubble.

I didn't know anything about barbed-wire fences or wheat, so it was fascinating to me to listen and try to envision what my Dad and Dale Simmons were discussing.

Now and then I caught a few words of the conversation between Mom and Mrs. Simmons. Theirs had turned mostly to summer canning of vegetables, fruits, jellies, and cutting up chickens for the freezers for winter. And also recipes they had found in the newspapers or in magazines that they had tried and liked.

I sipped my tea as I listened. I felt completely out of place. But still it was good to be home.

Dale Simmons finally looked over at me and then back at my Dad and asked Dad, "Have you seen that stallion your son brought home, Andy?"

"No," Dad answered. "He was still unloading him when I came in, and I didn't really pay much attention to his horse."

Getting up from the chair he was sitting in, Mr. Simmons waved an arm toward Dad and said, "Come on down to the corral and get a good look at him then."

Dad and I both got up and walked with Dale Simmons to the corral where Gunner was looking around at the pasture outside. When we got to the rails of the corral, I whistled, and Gunner walked to me. I climbed into the corral with him, petted him a few minutes, walked him a ways, and then turned him and walked him back to where Dad and Dale Simmons stood admiring him from the rails of the corral.

"That's some horse," Dad commented. "Where did you get him, James?"

I told Dad about working for Grant Rayes on the Slant T ranch near Miami, Oklahoma and about how Mr. Rayes let me work other jobs when the ranch work was slow. I had saved almost everything I earned. I told him that when I broke Gunner to ride, Mr. Rayes had let me buy Gunner from him.

"I've heard of the Slant T. I didn't know you were working there. He raises horses as well as cattle, doesn't he?" Dad asked me.

"Yes, and he also raises mules," I answered.

"Mules? What for?" Dad asked.

"I understand he has some sort of contract with the US Army," I told him.

"Interesting," Dale Simmons remarked.

"I thought maybe we could pick up a couple of mares to breed him to," I said, still petting Gunner.

"That's an idea, but right now, there's not much money in horses. That could change in coming years. If the market goes up, then it might be worth a try," Dad told me.

"Gunner can still use some training with working cattle," I replied. "Maybe by the time I get him trained for cattle and roping . . . well, who knows? Maybe by then the market will be back up."

Dale Simmons came up with an idea.

"There are men who will pay to have their horses trained for cattle and roping, James," Mr. Simmons said. "You might think of doing that when you get your horse trained like you want him."

"Thanks, Mr. Simmons. That is something to consider," I said.

Dad agreed with me and commented, "There's money in setting up a horse clinic, James. In fact, that's something both of us could work at doing when the ranch work is slow here."

Dad's gelding was working his way toward the corral, and Dad had me let Gunner out.

Watching the gelding and Gunner get acquainted reminded me of the day I rode in to the Hargrove place and found Humphry watching the four foals play.

I hadn't realized I had muttered aloud "Humphry didn't do it!" until Dad asked me, "Who is Humphry?"

"The most lovable kid in the world, Dad. I wish you and Mom and all of you could meet him. He doesn't know a stranger. In fact, when I stopped in to get some water for Gunner and fill my canteen, his mother got after him for talking to a stranger, and he told her I wasn't a stranger, I was James, and I was his friend," I told him.

Dad and Dale Simmons both smiled, and their eyes twinkled.

"Humphry is five, a little chubby, but with a beautiful smile that grabs your heart and a personality to match," I continued. "He is just the opposite of his older brother, Wayne, who is fourteen and lazy as all get out. And his mother has a hateful, sarcastic attitude that could put sarcasm to shame. I never did catch her name. But I wish you guys could meet little Humphry."

"Maybe someday we can," Dad replied. "You seem to be quite taken by this boy."

"Yes, I guess I am. And if you ever meet him, you will be taken in by him too," I assured him.

"How long do you intend to stay home?" Dad asked.

"As long as you need me here. I can go back to the Slant T anytime and still have a job there," I told him.

"Must be nice to have a job like that," Dale Simmons remarked. "Most folk like to have an estimated time of your absence."

"I know," I agreed. "But Mr. Rayes is a different sort of person. He just figures if I am not there, I have a reason for being away, and he just doesn't seem to worry about it one way or another."

"That's the job you need to be keeping," Dad commented.

"Well, I guess we better be getting back to our place," Mr. Simmons said.

We went back to the house where Mom and Mrs. Simmons were still visiting. I don't know how women find so much to talk about, but they seem to have an endless stream of conversation when they're together.

"Janet, you ready to go?" Mr. Simmons asked his wife.

"I'm coming," she told him as she and Mom walked outside and toward the Simmons pickup. There, hugs were given in friendship and the exchange of "see ya later" passed between them

After they left, we went back into the house. Mom had baked cinnamon rolls earlier in the day. Now she took them out of the pan and asked Dad and me if we wanted one. Of course we did! We both loved Mom's cinnamon rolls. That was one of the things I had missed about being gone. I savored the one I was eating now. I had forgotten how good they really are.

"Tomorrow we'll go check into this new winter wheat and maybe order some of it. Then we'll go find out how much the wheat drills run and a one-way plow," Dad told me. "That just sounded like a good idea while Dale and I were talking about it."

"Okay. And what about the combine the two of you were talking about?" I asked him.

"I don't know if they will have combines in as yet, but we can find out," Dad answered.

"If we have time, could we maybe look at some good used pickups?" I asked.

I figured when I left, if I had a vehicle, I could leave Gunner with Dad and Mom. Plus, if Mrs. Hargrove would let him come with me, I could bring little Humphry out to visit for a few days. Mom and Dad would love him just like I do.

I think Dad read my thoughts. He gave me a knowing look and told me we'd try to work it in to look at good used pickups and see if we could find what I wanted.

"Thanks, Dad," I told him.

If I could find a good-condition used pickup, I could also help haul fencing supplies for the fences Dad and Mr. Simmons planned to put in, and that would allow us to finish the fencing sooner. That would let me get back to check on Humphry sooner before I went back to the Slant T. I could only hope the little guy was okay.

The next morning, Dad and I went into Guymon and checked farm machinery place. Dad inquired about a grain drill and was told they only had two on the lot, but if neither of them were what he wanted, they could order one for him. I knew nothing about grain drills, but I followed Dad and the salesman to the ones on the lot.

One was a John Deere brand that spread out to ten feet. It had little disks that followed as it dropped the grains into the soil. The salesman recommended it to Dad over the other one, which was a brand he was not familiar with. It was from a new company, he said. Dad looked the John Deere one over thoroughly. He asked the salesman the price of it.

"I want to go check out that new wheat some of the folks are talking about. Can I have you hold this one for me until I do that? If the wheat looks good, I'll order some, and then I'll be back to talk to you some more about this drill," Dad told the salesman.

"Sure, Mr. Cotton. I really don't think it will go anywhere. But I'll post a note with your name on it until you decide one way or the other," the salesman answered him.

I marveled at how Dad could just ask for items to be held for him and the salesmen were agreeable. Dad had lived in this area for a long lot of years. People knew him and trusted him. I hoped someday I would have people knowing me that well.

He drove next to the local co-op. Here he inquired about the new strain of winter wheat.

He introduced me to Garrel Thompson who owned the co-op.

"I'm proud to meet you," I told him.

He smiled and turned back to Dad.

"Let me show you some of this new winter wheat. It comes from Canada, and some of the folks around here think it will do well down here," he said as he stopped and opened a gunny sack and scooped out a handful to show Dad.

Dad took it and looked it over, turned it into his other hand, and as he handed that handful back to Mr. Thompson, he asked him, "How much does this cost per bag?"

"It runs $3.52 per hundred pounds. But they add shipping charges, so probably we are looking at possibly $4.50 a bag. Maybe a little less," Mr. Thompson told Dad.

"Well, let's order me ten bags of it to try. If I don't like it, I can turn the cattle in on it. They eat about anything, especially something with grain heads on it," Dad told him.

Mr. Thompson laughed and told Dad to come on into the office with him while he made out the order for the Canadian wheat. Once inside his office, Mr. Thompson filled out an order form with Dad's name and phone number.

"I'll call you when it gets here," he assured Dad.

Dad shook hands and told him, "Thanks."

We went back to the farm machinery place. The salesman met us at the door.

"Well, how'd it go?" he asked Dad.

Dad pushed his hat back on his head a little farther and said, "I guess I need to buy that drill. I ordered ten bags of that Canadian wheat to try out. It looks to be pretty good."

"I'm glad to hear that," the salesman replied. "Do you mind if I tell people you think it looks pretty good?"

"Sure, go ahead," Dad agreed. "Now about that drill . . ."

The salesman looked embarrassed but went to the counter and pulled out a receipt he had already filled in while we were gone.

He placed it in front of Dad, along with an ink pen and told him, "I just need you to sign here, Mr. Cotton."

"You were pretty sure of me, weren't you?" Dad asked, chuckling, as he also took his checkbook out of his shirt pocket and wrote out a check for the drill.

"Thank you, Mr. Cotton. Now if you will bring your pickup around, we can get your drill attached to it," the salesman told my Dad.

We went to the pickup, and Dad pulled around to the drill.

"We really need a trailer to haul that home on. Do you happen to have a trailer on hand?" Dad asked the salesman.

"No. I'm sorry, Mr. Cotton. The best I can do is let you have a couple of red flags to attach to the back of it," he said.

Dad put the red flags at even intervals across the back of the drill. At least that would warn traffic he was pulling a wide load. He also asked for a red flag for the front of the pickup. That one he put in the middle of the pickup hood latch and anchored it with the hood itself. I was sure that was to warn oncoming traffic of the wide load also.

Dad got us home without any accidents. The few cars we met pulled a way over to let Dad pass. I saw Mom open the front door a little so she could see what Dad brought home. She waited until Dad got it maneuvered next to the hay bailer before she came out to look at his new machine.

"That's nice, Andy. I take it you bought some of that new wheat?" she commented.

"It looks to be good wheat. I ordered ten bags of it. I figured if it doesn't make like folks think it will, I can always turn the cows in on it," he answered her.

He put an arm around her and walked her back to the house. I followed along behind them.

"What do you plan to do this afternoon?" she asked Dad.

"I thought James and I can start building that new fence," he told her.

He took his straw hat off and hung it on a set of antlers he had mounted on the wall years ago.

"I baked a chicken casserole for lunch. If you two will go get washed up, we can eat," she told us.

I hadn't realized I was hungry, but the smell of that chicken casserole sure woke up my hunger buds.

Dad and I washed and sat down at the table. Dad said grace, and then we began to eat. I was glad Mom made plenty because her child was hungry enough for two people—more like famished.

When we were through eating, I went with Dad to start the fence. Mom said she was going to make bread and a pan of cinnamon rolls.

It had been a long time since I had built any fence. I think this new barbed wire was as new to Dad as it was to me. We set the posts we needed first, then strung the wire and pulled it tight, using a come-along and the pickup. Then we stapled it to the posts we had set. It looked nice when we got through with it. Dad was a stickler for fences being straight, even before barbed wire came along. Looking down along it brought back memories of Humphry, and before I knew it, I was telling Dad about me and Mr. Sweney fixing Mrs. Hargrove's pasture fence while Humphry took care of Gunner.

"He sounds like quite a kid," Dad commented.

"He is, Dad. He's the kind of kid that makes you want to be around him," I replied.

Then I went on to tell Dad about letting Humphry ride Gunner and about letting him drive the wagon back home after we took Sweney back to town.

I finished by stating, "At least he has a couple of good memories to cling to."

Dad agreed and gave me a fatherly, understanding look.

He didn't talk any more until we got home. I helped him put up the fencing tools, and we walked to the house together. I don't know for sure which of us was more anxious to bite into Mom's warm homemade bread. We spread it with butter and ate it before we took on any of the rest of supper. Afterward, we both ate a couple of cinnamon rolls. One was never enough. Mom's cinnamon rolls were to die for!

9

That night, that little rascal Humphry haunted my sleep. I kept hearing him tell me, "You hurry up and get back here, James!"

And I kept hearing him tell his mother, "He's not a stranger. He's James, and he's my friend!"

Finally, I did doze off, and when the alarm clock shook me awake, I felt like I had just laid down. I guess I probably managed a couple of hours' sleep. But I wasn't even ready to get up and face today.

When I dressed and stumbled into the kitchen, Mom had already made a pot of coffee and was fixing breakfast.

She looked at me and commented, "You look like you've been run over by a Mack truck, and I'm not so sure he didn't back up and run over you the second time."

I started to tell her "I must look like I feel then"; instead, I managed a smile and told her "good morning."

Dad came in a few minutes later. Mom set a cup of coffee down in front of him.

"What are you planning for today, Andy?" Mom asked.

"I'm going to plow that area James helped me fence off for this new wheat. He can go help Dale Simmons finish his fencing," he told her.

I wasn't sure I liked that idea, but Dad's word was law here at home. And realizing that I didn't know how to get to Dale Simmons' place, he told Mom she could drive me over there and stay and visit with Janet if she wanted to.

HUMPHRY DID IT!

After breakfast, I gathered my hat and my gloves and joined Mom at the pickup. Mom was happy to be getting away from home for a few hours. She didn't talk much on the way over to visit with Janet Simmons. She did ask me about Humphry as Dad had mentioned him to her. So I told her about Humphry and his easygoing ways and that beautiful smile of his and about him telling his mom that I wasn't a stranger, I was James, and I was his friend. I told her about Humphry going with me and Mr. Sweney to fix the pasture fence and about letting him ride Gunner on the way back to the corral and about letting him drive the wagon back home after we dropped Mr. Sweney off in town. I also elaborated about how sarcastic his mom was and how lazy his older brother, Wayne, was.

"You'd love him, Mom," I concluded.

She smiled and nodded a slight nod and agreed that she probably would love him.

After a few minutes, she suggested, "Maybe when you go back, you can talk his Mom into letting you bring him out here for a couple of weeks."

Her words shocked me. I hadn't thought about going back there even though Humphry invaded my thoughts during the day and my haunted my sleep at night. I had only intended to visit Mom and Dad and return to my job with Grant Rayes at the Slant T near Miami, Oklahoma.

"I don't know, Mom. That woman can embarrass the word *sarcastic* when she talks—or, should I say, *yells*. I don't think she knows how to speak without yelling. I mean, I know she has faced some hard times, but so have a lot of other folks. I paid her grocery bill and bought her some groceries. Then I bought a small freight wagon and bought what Mr. Sweney and I needed to fix her pasture fence so we could let the horses out to graze and to exercise. She had her mares penned up in her barn and was only feeding them a handful of grain every day. She even ordered me and Mr. Sweney both off her place. We just refused to leave until after we got the fence patched up," I confessed to Mom.

"But you were going back by there when you leave to go back to Miami, weren't you?" she asked me.

"I hadn't meant to, but it would be a good idea, I guess, for me to check on Humphry. By then, his mom will probably be in need of more groceries," I said.

"Maybe by the time you get back by there, she won't be so hateful," Mom commented.

"Maybe," I agreed.

I doubted it. I hoped that she had sure enough set her foot down with that oldest boy. And I hoped too that little Humphry wasn't having to still live under a daily ration of "Humphry did it!"

Mom didn't say any more until we got to the Simmons place where Mrs. Cotton and Mrs. Simmons exchanged hugs and greetings.

"Where's Dale?" Mom asked Mrs. Simmons.

"Oh, he's out trying to put up a fence," Mrs. Simmons answered.

"Well, get in and show us where he is because I brought James to help him work on that fence," Mom said.

Mrs. Simmons gave Mom directions to where her husband was building his new fence.

He stopped working when we drove up and came over to inquire why we had come out there.

"I brought James over to help you put up that new fence," Mom told him.

I got out of the pickup, and I walked around to where Dale Simmons was standing.

"It's good of you to help, James, but where's your dad?" he asked.

"Dad is plowing up a field that he intends to plant some of that new Canadian wheat in," I told him. "Dad bought a drill yesterday and ordered ten bags of that wheat."

Dale Simmons raised his eyebrows and commented, "I see. Well, let's get to work and get some fence put up. With you here to help me, we might just get it done before sundown."

"We'll be at the house if you need anything," Mom called out as she turned the pickup and headed back to the Simmons' house.

Mr. Simmons already had quite a few of his posts set. I helped him set the rest. Afterward, we strung the wire. Unlike Dad, he didn't have a come-along. I watched as he made a loop in the wire at the end of the fence and twisted it. Then he took a short strand of wire and looped it through the loop in the fence wire and twisted that one, linking the wires together. After that, he tied the end of the shorter piece around his bumper hitch at the back of his pickup and told me to get in while he stretched the wire taut. It didn't take much movement to stretch the wire as much as he wanted it. Then we stapled it to the posts and repeated the process on each of the next three wires.

I asked him why he had me get inside the vehicle each time he went to stretch a wire. I could have just stood back out of the way, I thought. And I said as much to Dale Simmons.

He looked at me and smiled, and then in a serious tone, he told me, "Son, if one of those wires had snapped while I was pulling them tight, the safest place for both of us was inside this pickup. Had you just stood to one side thinking you were out of the way and a wire snapped, it could have cut you to ribbons. Those barbs are sharp, and when a wire that has been stretched tightly enough to break, it usually wraps around anything near it and sinks those barbs in deeply as it wraps around its victim. I have no desire to have to cut you loose from the grip of barbed wire and hope you don't bleed to death before I can get you undone from it."

I must have looked dumbfounded because Mr. Simmons reached over and patted my shoulder and told me, "You did fine this afternoon, James. But don't ever forget that safety comes first in doing any job, be it fencing or some other."

"Yes, sir," I answered.

"Barbed wire," he went on, "is made to keep livestock in the pasture they're supposed to be in. The theory is that once they touch those barbs, it will let them know to stay where they belong. In that respect, it can be a friend and something to be respected at all times. But by the same token, you have to remember that it can be deadly if a body gets entangled in it."

"Thank you, Mr. Simmons. I'll remember that," I said.

Even Dad hadn't told me that.

I guess it just didn't occur to Dad that I didn't know about the dangerous side of barbed wire. I suppose he thought that because Mr. Sweney and I had fixed Mrs. Hargrove's fence that I already knew about the barbed wire. I appreciated Mr. Simmons telling me about its dangers.

I offered to come back the next day and help him again.

"That's good of you, James. We may have another three days of fencing, and it will go a lot faster with both of us working on it," he said.

"Would you like me to bring Dad's come-along tomorrow?" I asked.

"It's just as easy to tighten the wire the way I did today, James. And then I won't have to worry about breaking your dad's come-along," he answered. "'Course, if your dad is where he can come too, it would help us get through a little faster."

10

That evening, I told Dad I was going back the next day to help Dale Simmons put in more of his fence.

"Let's both go," he said. "That way, we can get his fence done and out of the way."

I nodded in agreement. I didn't know how much more fence Mr. Simmons had left to build, but with all three of us working, we could get it done a lot faster.

I went down by the corral to see Gunner and brush him down. Gunner was out in the pasture a ways, but when I whistled for him, he came. Dad's gelding wasn't far behind him. I brushed Gunner first, then Dad's gelding.

The clouds overhead were darkening, and the air smelled of rain. Here and there streaks of lightening played from the clouds to the ground. Then I saw smoke not too distant from the corral. I went back and told Dad. He came outside, and I pointed to the smoke. He told me to open the corral gate. He still had the plow hooked up to the tractor, and he brought the tractor through the corral.

I closed the gates and stepped onto the tractor with him. It was maybe three-quarters of a mile where the lightning had caused the grass to catch fire. Fortunately, there was no wind to drive it, and Dad was able to use the plow to stop the fire from spreading. It left an oblong, black blemish on the pasture; but it was a small area, and at least the whole pasture hadn't burned. By the time we got back to the house, it had started to sprinkle lightly.

"What was that all about, Andy?" Mom asked Dad.

He hadn't told her why he left the house so suddenly, and she didn't know where he was going with the tractor and plow. He took time to explain to her that the lightning had set a small area of grass on fire out in the pasture where the horses were. But he was able to plow it under and get it stopped.

"It's a good thing you saw it when you did," she commented.

"Tomorrow," he told her, "I'm going with James over to Dale's place and help them finish the fence Dale is putting in. So we'll be leaving early."

It sprinkled for almost an hour. But the ground was not so wet as to curtail fencing the next day.

* * * * *

Dad and I were up before the crack of dawn, and shortly thereafter, we were on our way to the Simmons ranch.

Dale Simmons was up and loading wire and fencing supplies into his vehicle when we got there. He and Dad shook hands, and Mr. Simmons told Dad he was glad Dad had come along. Today he had to fence the other three sides of the square mile he and I had finished the day before. This morning, while he and Dad worked the posthole diggers, I was appointed to set the posts and tamp them solidly in place. This effort took us until just after noon.

We stopped and went to the house for lunch. Mrs. Simmons had cooked a roast which she served with mashed potatoes and green beans and homemade dinner rolls. When we finished eating, Dad asked Mr. Simmons if he wanted to get in a mile of barbed wire fence this afternoon and then finish the other two miles tomorrow.

Mr. Simmons liked Dad's suggestion. So we went back out and put wire on a connecting mile of fence that afternoon before Dad and I went home.

When we got home, it was getting late. I went to check on Gunner. I didn't see him. I figured he and the gelding were out in the pasture somewhere grazing, so I went on up to the house.

"James your dad tells me that you and he will be at the Simmons place again tomorrow to help Dale finish the fence he is working on," Mom remarked as I entered the house.

"Yeah, we still have two more miles of wire to string," I answered.

"Maybe this weekend, he can plow the field again that he wants to plant the new wheat in," she commented.

"Maybe," I replied.

After a few minutes, Dad came out of the shower, and I took his place. It felt good to be washing today's sweat and dust from my body and then to be getting into clean clothes.

As I dressed, the vision of Humphry came to me. It was as though he were reaching out to me and calling me to hurry back. The vision shook me, and I stayed in the bathroom a few extra minutes to regain my composure before I joined Mom and Dad in the living room.

I didn't fool anyone. As I came into the room, Dad looked at me and asked, "Humphry?"

I nodded. Dad smiled, and so did Mom. But they didn't say anything further. I felt a little embarrassed that my emotions showed. And this was one of the few times I could admit that "Humphry did it!" That sweet little kid had stolen my heart.

Had he been any other kid, I would have gotten over him by now. But Humphry wasn't any other kid. He was that easygoing five-year-old with those sparkling eyes, that beautiful smile, good personality, and the kid who had told his mother, "He's not a stranger. He's James. And he's my friend." That same chubby little boy who had hollered at me as I was riding away to hurry up and come back.

How does one forget a kid like that?

Mom, as if she was reading my mind, asked, "When do you think you'll go back, James?"

"Not for a few days, Mom. I need to help Dad and Mr. Simmons finish the fences. And if Dad has some other things for me to help him with, we'll catch those up too," I told her. "I was thinking of looking for a good used pickup to drive back to Miami and leave Gunner here for a while. Dad's gelding is getting on in years, so he might need Gunner before I get back again."

Dad had been listening. Now he smiled. But he said nothing.

Dad and I got up early again so we could help Mr. Simmons get the other two miles of wire attached to the posts. And even though we got an early start, it was still just past noon by the time we finished the fence.

On the way back to the Simmons house, Dad told Mr. Simmons that he and I were going to go car shopping this afternoon to see if we can find a decent, good used pickup for me.

"The boy plans to leave his stallion with me for the winter, and I'd sure hate to see him have to walk back to Miami," Dad told Dale Simmons.

Dale Simmons joined in on the joshing, saying, "You know, Andy, he might just make it by spring. He'd get there in time to turn around and walk back and help you with the spring planting."

I smiled, and they both chuckled. It felt good to hear their laughter. I had always thought all grown-ups wore a serious look. I guess they did a mite more worrying than us younger folk do. They had a good deal of responsibility. Us young folk just had to grow up and leave home before we met up with responsibility and learned its true meaning.

*****

True to his word, Dad took me to Guymon the next morning, and we walked through all the vehicles they had on their lots. We were fixing to leave the last lot when I spotted a pickup off toward one corner that I wanted to look at. It was a Chevrolet that looked to be in excellent condition. It had black interior that set off its red exterior. It had an eight-foot bed and good tires. And it was low mileage. I liked it, and the more he looked at it, the more Dad liked it too.

I asked the salesman, "How much are you asking for this vehicle?"

"Thirty-eight hundred," he answered.

"What's wrong with it?" I asked.

The salesman looked surprised and told me there was nothing wrong with it and further explained it had belonged to an elderly lady who had told him to sell it and she didn't care about the price.

Before I could open my mouth Dad said, "We'll take it."

We followed the man into the dealership office where he filled in a sales contract. Dad had him put the pickup in my name, and afterward, he made out a check for it. The man ran Dad a copy of the contract and a copy of the check he had written.

He handed them to Dad with the keys to the vehicle and told Dad, "It was a pleasure doing business with you, Mr. Cotton."

Dad thanked him and handed me the keys to the pickup he had just bought.

I followed Dad home. When I got out of my new red pickup, I thanked Dad and told him, "I'll send you my checks from the Slant T until I get you paid back."

"No," Dad said. "You can pay me half your wages every month, but not all of them. You're going to need something for yourself. And by paying me half, you will eventually get this pickup paid for."

I told him okay, and then we looked under the hood and checked the fluids. Everything was clean so I wouldn't have to worry about that for a while.

Mom had seen us drive in, and she was now there at the red pickup with us listening to Dad explain all about it.

11

I spent two more weeks with Mom and Dad before heading back to my job down near Miami on the Slant T. Deep down, I really didn't want to leave. Helping Dad—and, at times, Dale Simmons also—was something I enjoyed. And I knew I was going to miss my Mom's cooking. If I had been a judge having to judge her cooking, she would have won a first-prize blue ribbon at every meal.

But I had a job waiting, and I knew I needed to get back to it. I have to admit, though, that after spending a few weeks at home with Mom and Dad, my job at the Slant T wasn't nearly as appealing as it had been years ago when I left home and found the job with Grant Rayes. Still, I knew it was time to go. So I said my goodbyes to my parents, gave Mom a hug, and shook hands with Dad and thanked him one more time for buying the pickup for me. Then I headed east in a direction that would bring me to the roads and highways I needed to travel to get back to Miami, Oklahoma.

Funny thing, I realized I had not missed the Slant T or the other cowboys I worked with the whole time I had been gone. And for some reason, I wasn't in any particular hurry to get back to them. And knowing I needed to didn't do a thing to get me to hurry back to them.

As I drove, I really didn't think of anything for a long while. Finally, I had to stop for gas and the restroom. I picked up some snacks and a bottle of water before I went back to the pickup and started once more toward the east.

I opened the candy bar and started to eat it as I drove. Immediately, little Humphry entered into my realm of thought. I wondered how the little guy was. I hoped he was okay. A couple hours later, I turned off the highway onto a dirt road that led to the place where Humphry lived. Forty-five minutes later, I pulled into the yard at Mrs. Hargrove's place.

I wasn't prepared for what I saw. The house had burned during my absence and the corral was in shambles. The little freight wagon was gone, and that left me to hope Mrs. Hargrove and her boys had escaped the burning house.

For some reason, I had the urge to call out for Humphry, and I did. I waited a few minutes and called his name again. Then I walked out to the barn, and as I neared it, I called again. I had just turned to walk back to my pickup when I heard a slight noise in the hayloft.

"Humphry, is that you?" I called out.

I was looking up in the direction I had heard the sound.

Seconds passed, and then I saw him peering over the edge of the loft.

"Humphry, what are you doing up there?" I asked him.

"James! You came back!" he exclaimed and started down the ladder from the loft.

When his feet touched the floor, he ran to me and threw his arms around me, still muttering, "James! You came back!"

I knelt and hugged him to me. He was trembling, so I just held him for a few minutes.

Then I took him by the shoulders and held him back a few inches so I could look into his face and asked him, "Humphry, what happened here?"

His face looked like he had lost his last friend. He was close to tears when he answered, "I didn't do it, James. Honest, I didn't."

"I believe you, Humphry, but what is it that you didn't do? Tell me what happened here," I prodded.

Slowly, little by little, Humphry told me his brother Wayne had come home sometime after dark three days ago. His mother had lit into him, and he hit her and knocked her against the table.

"Then what happened?" I asked.

"When Mama fell against the table, it fell and the lamp broke, and the dress Mama had on caught on fire. I got some water to put the fire out, but Wayne grabbed me and threw me outside. Then some other things caught on fire. Wayne wouldn't let me back in the house."

He paused and brushed away some tears that had started running down his cheeks.

"I told him we had to get Mama out of the house, but he was mad at her, and he wouldn't let me try to get her out, James."

His voice broke, and I hugged him to me again. I could only imagine in my mind's eye what this child had witnessed that night and the horror of having to watch the house burn down around his mother because of his worthless brother. I tried to control the anger that was beginning to surge through my body.

"What happened to the wagon, Humphry?" I asked him when he quieted down some.

"Wayne took it and Rosebud and took off. I don't know where he was going. And he didn't come back home," Humphry told me.

Learning this five-year-old boy had been alone for the past three days and without food really fanned the flames. It was probably a good thing his brother wasn't here right now.

I took my neck scarf off and wiped Humphry's face. Then I picked him up and carried him to my pickup. I still had some chips left that I hadn't eaten. I gave them to the boy.

"We'll go to town and get you some clothes, and then we'll go eat," I told him.

He said okay, and the chips disappeared quickly. I don't think he even breathed while he ate them. I think he inhaled them.

I stopped at the merchandise store where I found Jeffery Bowers busy straightening up his shelves. I told him I need to get Humphry a couple of sets of clothes and a pair of boots or shoes.

He took one look at Humphry, nodded, and asked what happened. I explained as well as I could what Humphry had told me. He was as shocked as I had been. He picked out two new outfits for Humphry and a pair of boots for him.

"Has anyone looked to see if they could find Mrs. Hargrove's body in the burned out house?" he asked.

"I doubt it seriously, Mr. Bowers. I just got back about an hour ago, and Humphry said it happened about three days ago. The older boy took off with the wagon and left him there by himself. But by then, it was too late to try to get his mother out of the house. I need to get him fed and get a shovel and see if I can find her body and bury her," I told him.

He shook his head.

Then he told me to go on and feed Humphry and he'd go get Mr. Sweney to go with us. He wouldn't let me pay him for the clothes for Humphry or for the shovel.

I walked with Humphry to the café and ordered meals for both of us.

I had to caution Humphry to take his time eating so his food would stay down. He had not eaten in three days, and his stomach might not take well to him eating too fast. He took his time, and I was glad he had listened to me.

When he was full, he asked, "James, where's Gunner? You didn't sell him to buy that pickup, did you?"

"No, son, I didn't sell Gunner. I left him with my Dad. My Dad bought me the pickup, and I have to pay him back from my wages when I get back to my job," I told him.

He gave me a serious look and asked in a pleading tone, "Can I go with you, James?"

"I will have to find out about that, Humphry. I'll have to find a sheriff or a judge or somebody who can give me legal permission to take you away from here. Otherwise, I could be accused of kidnapping you. That means taking you without permission and maybe against your will, in your brother's opinion or someone else's opinion."

"But I want to go with you, James. You're my friend," he replied.

"I'll do everything I can to get them to let you go with me. But I can't make you any promises," I told him honestly.

When he was through eating, we walked back to the merchandise store, and I asked Mr. Bowers who I would see about letting Humphry go with me.

He and Mr. Sweney looked at each other, and then Jeffery Bowers said, "You'd have to go on into Buffalo and see if you can find a lawyer and see what he says. We don't have one here. We ain't even got a sheriff to ask."

"Okay, then let's get his mother buried, and I will see what I can do about getting a legal piece of paper putting him in my custody," I told them.

They nodded in understanding.

12

I parked at the courthouse and took Humphry with me to the sheriff's office. One of the lawmen there was a Tracy Hoffman. He asked me what he could do for me. I asked him who I needed to see in reference to getting legal custody of little Humphry.

"What do you mean by that?" he asked.

I explained the situation to him. He looked thoughtful for a few minutes, then told me to follow him and we could find out if the Judge was still in his office.

At the judge's office, he told me to wait outside a couple of minutes while he talked to the judge. The sign printed on the door read "Judge Henry Launders." I wondered what kind of a judge he was. Some judges were levelheaded and willing to help people. Others had a reputation as "hanging judges." I hoped Judge Launders was the former. It was a few minutes before the deputy came out and told me the judge would see us now.

The judge was an elderly gentleman with white hair and wire-rimmed glasses.

"The deputy told me about the situation you're in, and although it is highly irregular, I am going to give you a document to sign for custody of the boy," he said in a kindly voice. "I'll need your name, your address, and the boy's name, age, and birthday."

I introduced myself as James Cotton, employed by Grant Rayes of the Slant T ranch near Miami, Oklahoma. I told him the boy is Humphry Hargrove from over near Gate. I told him Humphry is five years old, but I wasn't sure of his birthday.

The judge looked over at Humphry and, in a gentle voice, asked him when his birthday is.

Humphry didn't hesitate to tell him, "My birthday is July 25th, sir. I'll be six years old then."

Judge Launders thanked him with a smile and wrote the information down on the document he was filling out. After which, he asked Humphry how he come to know me and if I was related to him.

"James is my friend!" Humphry spoke up proudly.

He went on to tell him how I had ridden on to his mother's place and asked to water my horse and how I had stayed a few days and fixed the pasture fence, bought his Mama groceries, cleaned out the barn for them, and bought a wagon and the mare that came with it so his mama didn't have to walk to town anymore. He went on to say that I had left because I had some business to do somewhere else.

"But I told him to hurry up and come back, and he did," Humphry added. "He just didn't get here before my older brother beat my mama and set the house on fire and ran off with the wagon. He wouldn't let me try to get mama out of the house, and he wouldn't let me go with him either. So I hid in the barn until James got back this morning."

"How old is your brother, Humphry?" the judge asked.

"Wayne? He's fifteen now. He never stayed home much, and he used to tell Mama that I did bad things when it was him that did them," Humphry told him.

The judge told the deputy to put out a statewide search for Wayne Hargrove. He asked me to describe him, and I did. Then he asked me my opinion of Wayne Hargrove.

"From what I saw of him, he's worthless and lazy," I told him.

He asked how to get to the Hargrove place, and I gave him directions. He told Deputy Hoffman to send someone out to check the place because Wayne may have gone back to the place.

"I want him brought in alive, if possible," the judge concluded.

He handed the document to me for a signature and date, had it notarized, and then printed off a copy for me to take with me. Then he shook hands with me and then with Humphry also. He wished us luck.

HUMPHRY DID IT!

I thanked him and Humphry thanked him; and we left the courthouse for my pickup, stopped at the gas station for fuel, and headed once more toward Miami.

Humphry was a happy child. His eyes sparkled. His smile took its place on his face.

"I knew you could do it, James!" he told me.

He knew more than I did. I was not at all sure the judge would sign custody of him over to me without a trial and legal proceedings. I had a feeling it was Humphry's story that swayed the judge and maybe the Deputy's story also in relating to the judge what I had told him in his office. I just hoped I could be the friend the child needed now.

On the way to Miami, Humphry went to sleep, and I let him sleep. There was no reason to wake him. He had endured more stress and heartache in the past week than any five-year-old had a right to have to endure. I knew he had to be exhausted. Now that the judge had granted me custody of him, he felt safe again.

It was sundown when I pulled into the ranch yard of the Slant T. I parked near the house because I wanted to talk to Mr. Rayes about having Humphry to care for now and to make sure it was okay to have him with me here at the ranch.

I left Humphry sleeping in the pickup and went up and knocked on Mr. Rayes's door.

In a moment, Mrs. Rayes answered. I asked her if the boss was in. She told me he was in his office and to come on back.

Mr. Rayes stood up and extended a hand for a handshake and commented, "Good to have you back, James. Come on in and sit down. How were your folks?"

"They're fine, but I have something else I need to talk to you about," I told him.

"You didn't go get married on me, did you?" he smiled.

"In a way, I guess I did," I said.

I took my hat off and held it in my hands.

Mr. Rayes gave me a questioning look and asked, "What do you mean 'in a way, you guess you did'? You either did or you didn't."

"I didn't, but . . ."

I told him the rest of the story from stopping for water at the Hargrove place to coming back to find the house burned, Wayne and the wagon gone, and Humphry hiding in the loft in the barn. And I went on to tell him about the judge at the Buffalo courthouse signing a document placing Humphry in my custody and telling the deputy he wanted Wayne brought in—alive, if possible.

"I want to know if it is all right to have Humphry here at the ranch with me, or if I need to take him back to Mom and Dad."

Mr. Rayes looked thoughtful for several minutes before he asked me gently, "Where is the boy now?"

"Asleep in my pickup right outside the house," I told him.

"Let's bring him in the house," he stated and asked his wife if she would get a bed ready for the child.

She nodded and left us.

I opened the pickup's passenger-side door. Humphry still slept. I lifted him carefully out of the pickup and turned to take him into the house.

Mr. Rayes held out his arms and said, "Let me."

I closed the pickup door and followed him inside where he went down the hall to a room at the end of it and laid Humphry very carefully onto the bed his wife had prepared. He looked down at Humphry as a father might look down at his own son. Then he carefully took off Humphry's boots and covered him up.

"You better sleep in this room tonight too, James, so if he wakes up, he won't be so scared at being in a strange place," he told me.

As we left the room Mrs. Rayes commented, "He's a cute little guy."

13

I was rolling up the pallet I had slept on when Humphry woke up. He sat up on the bed and told me, "James, I need to go pee."

"Okay, son, I'll show you where the bathroom is," I said.

I took hold of his hand and led him down the hall to the bathroom and closed the door behind us. He had never seen an indoor bathroom before, and he marveled at it with open admiration.

Pointing at the bath tub, he asked me, "What's that?"

I explained to him that it was called a bathtub and was where people took their baths.

"We need to give you a bath before we go eat breakfast," I told him. "I need to go out to my pickup and get your other set of clothes, and after your bath, you can put them on and be a clean boy. At breakfast, you will probably meet the other men I work with. They eat breakfast here in the main house sometimes. If they don't, then you will get to go outside and probably to the bunkhouse to meet them."

Humphry smiled and agreed, I think more to please me than anything else.

I walked him back to the bedroom and told him to stay there while I brought his clean clothes in.

Mrs. Rayes was already starting breakfast. I told her good morning and asked if it was okay if I gave Humphry a bath. She smiled and agreed. I got his clean clothes from the pickup and returned to the bedroom where young Humphry waited.

"Come on, sport, let's get you cleaned up," I told him, and he followed me to the bathroom.

I turned on the water to fill the tub and told Humphry he had to completely undress, and after he shed his clothes, I helped him into the tub of warm water. I took the soap and scrubbed him down and rinsed him off, then had him get on his knees and lean forward so I could wash his hair.

"Close your eyes so I don't get soap in them," I told him.

Minutes later, I helped him dry off and get into his clean garments. I took the plug from the tub so it could drain. Then I took my comb from my shirt pocket and combed out his hair. I had him pick up his dirty clothes, and we walked back to the bedroom, laid his dirty clothes on the floor next to the bedhead, and I had him slip into his new boots. Then we walked down the hall to the kitchen table.

"My, don't you look nice!" Mrs. Rayes exclaimed, beaming at Humphry.

I introduced him to her and to Mr. Rayes who had followed us into the kitchen.

His eyes twinkled, and that beautiful smile took its place on his young face.

"Hi! James is my friend!" he said.

That brought a round of smiles from the rest of us.

Mrs. Rayes fixed Humphry a plate and set it before him, then brought him a glass of milk. Afterward, she did the same for the rest of us.

Humphry ate every bite and commented, "That was good, Grandma. You're a good cook."

Mrs. Rayes beamed, telling him, "Why, thank you, Humphry."

She didn't seem to mind that he had called her Grandma. Mr. Rayes chuckled.

He reached over and took Humphry by the hand and told him, "Let's go meet the rest of the men."

Humphry got up, and we went outside where the other men were already admiring my pickup.

As we came out on the porch, they gathered around in front of us.

"Whose pickup is this?" Bob Heather asked.

"Mine," I told him. "And this is my adopted son, Humphry."

HUMPHRY DID IT!

Why I had heard myself tell the men Humphry was my *adopted* son—I didn't know. The word had just slipped out.

I put a hand on Humphry's shoulder and introduced him to them, "Humphry, this is Bob Heather, Lyle Canton, Andy Tremmel, and Steve Dayton. I think you will like them all."

Humphry looked up at me and back at the men and gave them one of his beautiful smiles.

"Well, Hum, now that you've met the men," Mr. Rayes said, "we better let Grandma take you to town and get you some more clothes and see what else you need."

To his men, Mr. Rayes said, "I know this is a surprise, but I hope all of you will make the boy welcome and help him find things he can do to feel like he's helping out."

I handed Mrs. Rayes the key to my pickup and tried to give her some money to pay for whatever she thought Humphry needed. She refused the money, telling me she didn't need it and that she and Hum would do just fine.

As they were leaving, Humphry turned to Mr. Rayes and said, "Bye, Grandpa. We'll see you later!"

I didn't know what prompted Humphry to call Mr. and Mrs. Rayes Grandma and Grandpa. Maybe because they were likeable people. Neither did I know why my boss had shortened Humphry's name to Hum. Humphry seemed to like it, nonetheless. I had to admit, it went with his personality.

I caught myself saying, "Hurry home, Humphry!"

Andy Tremmel asked me where I had picked up Humphry, adding, "He seems like a nice kid."

The rest of the men agreed with Andy, and Grant Rayes allowed me to relay the story to them as to how I came into the custody of Humphry. I added that I don't know why Humphry had called Mr. and Mrs. Rayes Grandma and Grandpa.

Mr. Rayes spoke up and said, "I don't mind the kid calling me Grandpa, as long as he doesn't mind the rest of us calling him Hum instead of Humphry."

That brought a round of laughter from the men, along with agreeing nods. Mr. Rayes then told them to let the young new member of the Slant T help whenever he could and to look out for him. They assured him they would, and he ushered the orders for what they needed to be doing today. That included mending a fence on the north range.

I was sent with the crew to mend that and took a bit of joshing about coming home with a son, but I knew it for what it was when they teased me and called me "Daddy James" on and off during the day.

And then the thought hit me, and I responded to one of the "Daddy James" remarks with, "I guess that makes you all his uncles!"

That hit their funny bones, and they began ragging each other with "Uncle Bob," "Uncle Andy," "Uncle Lyle," and "Uncle Steve."

It made for a fun day at work, and Mr. Rayes was surprised to hear us coming back in that evening still teasing each other with "Daddy James" and "Uncle." Lyle filled him in on how the day had gone, and when he finished, even Mr. Rayes was laughing with us.

"Well, if you uncles will put things up, Daddy James needs to come in the house and see what Grandma Rayes bought his son today," he told them.

I followed him inside and down the hall where Humphry's new things lay across the bed.

Humphry gave me a hug and said, "Look what Grandma bought me, James! And she bought me some peppermint sticks too!"

Mrs. Rayes had bought him several long-sleeved shirts—a couple nice ones to wear to church—several pairs of new jeans and underwear and socks, a new belt, and a cowboy hat. I would be months paying her back for all the things she had gotten Humphry.

"Those are nice, Humphry. Try to take care of them," I told him.

"I will, James!" he said.

It was good to see this five-year-old—soon to be six—happy again. His eyes were sparkling, his smile heart grabbing, his personality back in place.

"Did you thank Mrs. Rayes for buying you these new clothes?" I asked him.

"Yeah, I did. I like Grandma Rayes, James." he told me.

I smiled and told him, "So do I, son. And the men don't mind if you call them uncle either."

"Really? I can call them uncle?" he asked.

HUMPHRY DID IT!

I had just made his day. He had found a whole new world.

Mr. Rayes smiled and, in a laughing tone, said, "Boys, we had best wash up for supper."

14

The next morning, Humphry asked Mrs. Rayes if there was something he could do to help out.

She stopped drying the dishes and said, "Come with me, Hum. I'll show you where we keep the chicken feed, and you can give them some grain and then gather the eggs for me."

Humphry's eyes lit up. You'd have thought Mrs. Rayes had handed him a brand-new silver dollar! Moments later, I saw him with a small galvanized bucket that he carried into the yard, and holding it with one hand, he used his other hand to scatter the grain for the chickens.

When the bucket was empty, he went to the inside of the chicken coop; and in no time, he emerged with the bucket, closed the chicken house door, and delivered the eggs to Mrs. Rayes in the kitchen.

She thanked him, and he asked her if he could get the chickens some water.

"Of course, Hum. I usually just dip some out of the trough at the well. There is a bucket we keep there in case we need to prime the well, so be sure you put it back after you give the chickens their water," she told him.

"Yes, ma'am," he answered.

And he set about dipping a bucket full of water and taking it to the chicken pen where he filled their shallow, little troughs for them. Then he replaced the bucket where it had been by the well. As he set the bucket down, Humphry spied Lyle Canton going into the blacksmith shed, and he followed.

"Morning, Uncle Lyle!" his cheerful voice rang out.

Lyle nodded to him and said, "Mornin' yerself, Hum."

"Whatcha doing, Uncle Lyle?" Humphry asked.

"I'm fixing to work on a broken harness," Lyle replied.

"Can I watch?"

"Sure ya can. Ya might even learn something if ya pay attention," Lyle told him.

"Thanks, Uncle Lyle! You sure are nice," Humphry told him.

Lyle brought out the harness he wanted to work on and set about being busy. Humphry watched in fascination. And that's how Mr. Rayes found them later on when he came to check on Lyle and see if he was about through with the harness. For a few minutes, he stood silently watching Lyle finish the harness and was surprised that Humphry, while watching Lyle intently, was not saying a word. He had been so quiet that Lyle had forgotten he was there.

"Are you helping Lyle fix that harness, Hum?" he asked.

Lyle looked up at Mr. Rayes and commented, "I'd forgotten he was here, boss. Most kids would have talked my ear off, but Hum has sat quietly and watched me work."

"Uncle Lyle does good work, Grandpa. Someday I want to be as good as he is," Humphry spoke up.

"And maybe you will be," Grant Rayes answered.

"I hope so, Grandpa," Humphry said.

That evening, when Bob and Andy and I came in from checking on the cattle over on the westernmost side of the ranch and checking the pond and the windmill over there, Humphry and Lyle were sitting on the porch outside of the bunkhouse. Lyle, who had never let anyone touch his guitar, was showing this chubby little five-year-old how to strum it and teaching him the chords.

Lyle was tall and lean, and he had Humphry sitting on the step below him and was reaching his long arms around the boy on either side to show him where to try to put his fingers on the strings. Humphry was paying attention with a serious expression on his face. We three sat our horses a few minutes watching. I wished I had a camera for this was a shot of a lifetime. But that's always when a person doesn't have a camera on hand.

After a few minutes, we put up our horses and decided to wash up and get ready for the evening meal. We spoke to Humphry and Lyle as we walked past them toward the house. Lyle nodded to us.

But Humphry was excited as he told me proudly, "Uncle Lyle is teaching me how to play his guitar, James!"

"I guess I better put the guitar up so we can go eat too," Lyle told him, as he rose carefully and took his guitar inside the bunkhouse.

Then he and Humphry walked together to the house.

After Mr. Rayes said grace, he began passing the food around the table. I asked Humphry what he had done today.

His eyes sparkled, and he smiled and told me, "Grandma showed me where the grain was for the chickens, and she let me feed them, then get water for them, and then she let me gather the eggs. And after that, I watched while Uncle Lyle worked on a harness. I hope I learn how to fix harnesses as good as he does. And after that, we cleaned out the barn. And then Uncle Lyle was teaching me how to play his guitar."

I don't think he even breathed as he told me what all he had done today. Everyone was smiling at his enthusiastic account of his day.

"It sounds like you had a busy day," I replied.

"Maybe," Mrs. Rayes suggested, "you could get him a guitar his size for his birthday. It's just a couple weeks away."

"That's a good idea," I told her.

I asked Humphry if he would like a guitar of his own. He had a mouthful of food, so he only nodded *yes* to my question.

I saw smiles touch the faces of the rest of the men, and looks passed between them. I had a distinct feeling this would be a birthday Humphry was destined to remember the rest of his life.

"Hum, you want to go with me tomorrow?" Mr. Rayes asked him.

"Sure, Grandpa. Where we going?" Humphry asked him.

"Oh, I thought we might ride out and look over the horses—that is, if you want to," Mr. Rayes told him. "You can help me pick out another one for James to train and maybe one he can train for you to learn to ride too."

"You mean it, Grandpa?"

Mr. Rayes smiled and told him, "Yes, Hum, I mean it. You're old enough to learn to ride. You're fixing to be six years old in a couple weeks. And once the horse is trained and you learn to ride it, you'll be able to ride with us men at times to check on the cattle and such."

"I want to learn to ride, Grandpa, like you and the others do. And maybe James can find a horse he can train like he did Gunner."

The kid was serious, and we all knew it.

* * * * *

The next morning, Humphry was up early. He fed and watered the chickens and gathered the eggs.

Mrs. Rayes was surprised to find the eggs on her counter when she went in to start breakfast.

Not thinking, she asked, "Who did this?"

"Humphry did it," her husband told her. "He was up early because he is excited about going with me today to see the horses."

"And of course you'll let him pick out one he likes and then bring it home for James to train," she sparkled as she said it.

He smiled. His wife knew him pretty well, plus she had heard him talking to Hum about it the evening before and knew he had asked if he wanted to go with him and pick out some horses for James to train.

"I think I may take Steve along too. He's pretty handy at roping and getting his newly caught horse to follow along behind him. He just seems to have a way with them, the same as James does at training them," he commented. "The rest can see about cleaning out the springs."

He had a couple of natural springs on his property, and he liked to check on them every once in a while to make sure they weren't clogged up.

When his hands were all seated around the table, he told them his plan and suggested the rest pair up and ride two together to check the springs and clean them out if they needed it. Steve was middle-aged, about five feet eight with a few extra pounds beginning to show. He was a good cowboy, and he knew horses as well as he did cattle. He didn't mind stepping back and letting me do the training on the horses. If I asked him about something, he would answer him, but other than that, he stayed out of the way and let me handle them.

Humphry was excited. He was ready to go. And with Uncle Steve going, that made it all the better. Grandpa Rayes was letting him ride a gentle mare.

The horses were on the east side of the ranch in a large pasture with rolling hills, scattered trees, and a windmill with a large water tank. There were forty-five horses on the pasture plus this year's foals. They were about every color you can imagine. Humphry's eyes widened, and so did his smile when he saw them.

"Well, Hum, look them over and see if you find one you want," Grant Rayes told him.

"Are all these horses yours, Grandpa?" Humphry breathed in astonishment.

Both Rayes and Steve laughed at him.

But Grant Rayes told him to pick out the one he wanted so Steve would catch it for him.

Humphry looked and laughed at the horses as they pranced and the babies played. Finally he chose a young perlino filly. Perlinos didn't usually get too tall. They were, as a rule, around fourteen hands high, sometimes fifteen hands high. She was a long two-year-old and a good pick for Humphry. Steve roped her. She fought for a few minutes before settling down to follow Steve as they rode back toward the ranch.

On the way, Steve remembered, "We didn't catch one for James."

"That's okay. James may want to pick his own," Mr. Rayes told him.

"What are you going to name your horse, Hum?" Mr. Rayes asked Humphry.

"I don't know, Grandpa. What do you and Uncle Steve think would be a good name?" Humphry asked.

"How about Frosty? Or Misty? Or Cloud? Or Pearl? Or something like that?" Steve suggested.

"Can I name her Lady?" Humphry wanted to know.

"That's a good name, Hum," Rayes told him. "She definitely looks like a lady."

"She sure is pretty," Humphry commented. "Just wait 'til James sees her!"

Back at the ranch, Steve put the young mare in the corral nearest the barn. He then unsaddled the other three horses and put them in with her. It didn't take long before the younger horse calmed down.

"Thank you, Grandpa, for giving me Lady, and thank you, Uncle Steve, for catching her for me," Humphry said, watching his new horse mill around the corral with the other horses.

"Uncle Steve, would you show me how to rope one of these days? I want to be as good at it as you are," Humphry said to the cowboy.

"Maybe later I can show you a few things about roping, button," Steve told him.

"We better knock off for now. It's almost lunchtime," Mr. Rayes told them.

"Do you have something you want me to do after lunch, Grandpa?" Humphry asked.

"Let's eat lunch first, then we'll see what we can dream up for you to do," Mr. Rayes replied.

15

When they were through eating, Mr. Rayes asked Humphry, "Hum, have you ever weeded a garden?"

"No, Grandpa. We never had a garden," Humphry answered.

"Well, come on, and I'll show you where the garden is and how to pull the weeds from around the vegetables," Mr. Rayes told him.

"Grant, you may have to water it and let him pull weeds tomorrow," his wife told him. "The ground may be too dry right now for him to pull the weeds."

"We'll go out and look it over," Rayes said, putting an arm around Humphry's shoulders and leading him toward the door.

The garden was big and on the north side of the house where it got both the morning and the afternoon sunlight.

"What all have you got in the garden?" Humphry asked.

"I don't know, just what all my wife planted, Hum. I know there's peas and carrots and green beans and potatoes and tomatoes. Maybe some turnips and some radishes and squash and cucumbers. And I wouldn't be surprised if she didn't plant some cantaloupe and maybe some watermelons," he told Humphry.

By now, they had reached the edge of the garden.

Having never seen a garden before, Humphry was amazed at how large it was and how it had been planted in rows that were evenly spaced to give the plants room to grow and to allow for a person to walk between the rows. At the front of each row was a marker that told what was planted in the row.

Mr. Rayes took the time to show the youngster what each vegetable and fruit plant looked like and also what the weeds looked like. He reached down and pulled a handful of weeds and checked the soil too. He had Humphry also pick up a bit of the soil and feel of it.

"This soil is a little dry, Hum. I think the wife was right. I best water it tonight and let you weed it tomorrow," he told the boy.

"Okay," Humphry said.

He could help Grandma by keeping the weeds out of the garden for her, and he liked that idea.

Later that evening, Mr. Rayes showed him where to turn on the garden sprinklers.

"We usually water the garden for about an hour in the evenings about every other day, Hum," he told Humphry. "Unless it rains. And if it rains, the garden doesn't need extra water again until the soil gets like it is now. And it only takes a few seconds to check the soil for moisture."

Mr. Rayes was pleased that Humphry had taken an interest in the garden. He would be a big help to Mrs. Rayes in picking what she needed out of the garden as the plants bore their individual fruits. He would later show Humphry how to dig the carrots and potatoes and turnips. And he would show him how to check the cantaloupe and watermelons for ripeness when it came time to start picking those. He himself liked fresh cut cantaloupe with his breakfast, and the tomatoes were a plus for lunch and supper.

* * * * *

Humphry's birthday was celebrated in the afternoon so all the hired hands could be there for it. There were a few wrapped packages that held new clothes he would be able to wear to school. And then there was a new saddle, blanket, and bridle that Steven and Andy had gone together to get him. There was a new Humphry-sized guitar with instruction guides for him to learn from that came from Lyle. Bob got a new halter and some leg wraps for little Humphry, and I had bought him a saddle rack and a package of peppermint sticks. Mrs. Rayes had baked and put together a triple-layer chocolate cake with chocolate icing and small birthday candles on top.

She had even managed to slip some vanilla ice cream past all of them and now served it with slices of cake after they had sang "Happy Birthday" to Humphry.

Humphry thanked each of the uncles for the gifts they had given him and gave each a hug also, embarrassing both Bob and Steven.

Then Humphry turned to me and asked, "James, would you help me find a place to put my new saddle and gear?"

His eyes were twinkling, and that ever-ready beautiful smile was in place, grabbing at my heart.

"Sure," I told him.

He then went to Mrs. Rayes, gave her a hug, and told her, "I love you, Grandma!"

He did the same thing to Mr. Rayes, saying, "I love you too, Grandpa!"

"And we love you, too, Hum," Grant Rayes told him.

It was amazing what being on the Slant T ranch these past few weeks had done for Humphry. And I think it had done a lot for Mr. and Mrs. Rayes also, as well as for the hands.

All of them felt something inside toward the boy. I had been afraid he wouldn't be allowed on the ranch and that I'd have to make other arrangements for him. I couldn't have been more wrong.

Humphry's personality blossomed. His charm soared. Unless you had experienced a few days of having spent time on the Hargrove place, you would never have known how bad life had been for him in his early years.

I think Mr. and Mrs. Rayes half expected him to be a little brat, to demand getting his own way, doing things deliberately to get attention like some of the kids who had previously visited the ranch at times. But despite his hard life, Humphry remained pleasant and likeable and a joy to be around. He never dipped into self-pity and seldom mentioned his former life. It was like he had shut the door on his past life.

I wasn't sure how the hired hands would treat him or take to him, but it didn't take them long to develop a liking for him. More and more they enjoyed being around him, and more and more they asked him if he wanted to help with a job. And they taught him how to do things the right way, even though he was still quite young. Was it any wonder they let him call them uncle?

After his birthday, he spent time every day to go to the corral and talk to his perlino mare.

That was always after he had finished whatever he was doing helping someone else do. She responded to him from the first day she had come home with him and Steve and Mr. Rayes. She calmed down quickly, and before the week was out, Humphry was able to get inside the corral with her where she let him pet her.

He found time also to be with Lyle in the evenings to learn to play his new guitar. He learned quickly, much to Lyle's amazement. And by the time it was time to enroll him in school, he could play couple songs, either by himself or with Lyle.

Bob and Steve both helped him learn how to rope. They were equally proud of his progress. Me, I worked mostly at breaking his new little mare Lady.

She wasn't too sure about the saddle. At first, she shied away from it. After that, she bucked it off a few times. But with a bit of coaxing, she finally stood and allowed me to saddle her. I walked her around the corral several times, still talking to her and then letting her stand tied to the corral for several minutes. Then I walked her some more. I unsaddled her and turned her loose. I put the saddle and the halter where they belonged.

The next few days, I repeated saddling her and walking her until I felt it was time to see how she would react to weight on the saddle. I used a gunny sack partially filled with sand at first to put across the saddle. She accepted the weight but tried to step away from me as I lifted it on to the saddle. I talked to her and petted her, and we walked around the corral, with her voicing her opinion every few steps during the first round. After realizing the sandbag wasn't hurting her, she quit neighing and settled down. We worked that way for a couple of days. Then one day I didn't bring out the sandbag, and Lady snickered as if to ask why I hadn't brought it this time.

"We don't need it today, girl. Today, it's going to be you and me," I told her.

She turned her head as I reached for the saddle horn and stuck my foot into the stirrup. When I pulled myself up onto the saddle,

I fully expected her to buck some. She didn't. I clucked to her and tapped her sides with my feet. It took her a few minutes to realize what I wanted her to do, but then she stepped out into a nice walk around the corral.

"Good girl, Lady," I told her.

I spent as much time with the perlino as I could while breaking in the other horses Mr. Rayes had sent Bob and Andy to bring back to the corrals. Steve helped with a couple of those also. Between fixing harnesses and such, Lyle kept busy riding line and keeping a check on the livestock, sometimes with one of the others, but more often than not he rode alone. No matter how long his day was, he always found time to be with Humphry in the evenings to teach the boy more and more how to play his guitar. Humphry ate it up. He loved the time Uncle Lyle spent with him, and he loved Uncle Lyle too.

Mrs. Rayes didn't have to worry about tending the chickens and gathering the eggs. There were times that her husband asked who had done those things, and she would answer, "Humphry did it!"

It was the same with the weeding and watering of the garden. Humphry loved the garden and watching the plants blossom and the fruits and vegetables grow. I think at times that was his little piece of paradise—time he could spend with himself and talk to the plants as he weeded, and he could talk to the bees that gathered the pollen from the flowering plants. In all the time he spent in the garden, he never got stung by the bees.

Mr. Rayes walked out to the garden one evening with his wife. He was surprised at how well everything was growing and producing. He asked Mrs. Rayes who had taken such good care of the garden, and she smiled and told him, "Humphry does it!"

"He has done a good job with it," Mr. Rayes commented.

"Yes, and I don't even have to ask him to do it. He takes care of the chickens in the morning for me and brings the eggs to the house without me having to ask him to do that either," Mrs. Rayes replied. "He seems to enjoy it, Grant."

He looked at her and smiled. He then reminded her that sometime next week, she needed to take both Humphry and me into town to see about getting Humphry enrolled in school.

That evening, at supper, Mr. Rayes brought up the subject of getting Humphry enrolled in school in the coming week. He asked me if I had worked with Humphry on his alphabet or his numbers. I had to admit I had not.

"Well then, I think for the next week, before school starts, you need to sit down with him for an hour every evening and teach him the alphabet and how to spell his name and how to read some. And maybe he can learn some of the numbers too. Maybe work at that for thirty minutes of numbers and thirty minutes of the alphabet," Mr. Rayes suggested.

I looked at Humphry and told my boss, "Okay."

"And I think you might want to enroll him as Humphry Cotton," Andy commented. "Folks around here won't know the difference, and it might save a lot of sarcastic remarks from other kids at school."

"Would you like that, Humphry?" I asked.

I got another of those wonderful smiles, and his eyes twinkled as he exclaimed, "Yes I would, James!"

"All right then. You are now Humphry Cotton. Better known here on the ranch as Hum Cotton," I told him with a smile.

Everyone else nodded in agreement, including Mr. and Mrs. Rayes.

16

School registration was on a Wednesday. Mrs. Rayes came with me to register Humphry and get him set up to start first grade in the Miami Elementary School. I registered him as Humphry Cotton and was much relieved that no one questioned us about registering him with that name. As Andy had said, most folks didn't know the difference anyway.

The only thing Mrs. Rayes and I worried about were the shots the woman doing the registering mentioned. But she said the school nurse would set aside a date for those to be given, and she would let us know when it was to be. I thanked her and asked her what all Humphry needed to bring with him the first day. She produced a short list and gave it to me.

"And," she said, "he can either bring a lunch or eat here at school, whichever you prefer."

I asked Humphry if he wanted to eat at school.

He was quick to answer, "No, I like Grandma's cooking. I'd rather bring my lunches."

Mrs. Rayes smiled, and so did the lady at the desk. I didn't blame him; Mrs. Rayes was a good cook.

The thought of good cooking reminded me of Mom and Dad. Humphry wouldn't get a chance to meet them until spring break. And I guessed if I didn't want to be disowned, I had better get a much-awaited letter written to them. I had meant to write them before now; I just hadn't gotten around to it. I vowed to myself I would make time this evening to get that done and maybe let Humphry write a few lines too, if he felt up to it.

HUMPHRY DID IT!

Humphry had done a pretty fair job of learning to print some words, say and print his alphabet and numbers, and learned a bit of reading these past two weeks. He had even laid aside his guitar practice to learn to try to read and write. We were all proud of him. And we could brag with pride that "Humphry did it!"

We left the schoolhouse and went by the store to get the school supplies Humphry needed. I also bought him some of the peppermint sticks he loved. Mrs. Rayes bought a few groceries she needed before we went back to the ranch.

Humphry was excited and went to find Mr. Rayes to tell him all about his day at the schoolhouse.

I helped Mrs. Rayes take her groceries in, and then I put Humphry's school supplies in his room.

"Mrs. Rayes, would it be all right if I go out to the bunkhouse and write a letter to my folks? I haven't written them since I got back," I asked her.

"Sure," she told me. "There's paper and envelopes and ink pens in the desk in the living room. Get what you need, James."

I did and carried my writing materials out to the bunkhouse. There was an oblong table there where we sometimes played card games or used it to put spare parts of whatever we were fixing on. It served as my writing desk.

I apologized for not writing sooner. Then I went on to tell them what I had come upon the Hargrove place and the judge in Buffalo granting me custody of Humphry and how Mr. and Mrs. Rayes had taken to him and allowed him to call them Grandma Rayes and Grandpa Rayes. I told them how the hired hands let him call them Uncle Andy, Uncle Bob, Uncle Steve, and Uncle Lyle and how they were teaching him how to rope and care for the horses and helped him with other chores and that Lyle had bought him a Humphry-sized guitar for his birthday that he was learning to play. I told them about Mr. Rayes taking him with him and letting Humphry pick the horse he wanted for his own, a perlino filly that I was breaking for him when I had time from training some of the horses for Mr. Rayes.

I told them how Humphry took over tending to the chickens and weeding the big garden Mrs. Rayes had planted and that how now when someone said "Humphry did it!" it was for something he had done good, not because they were looking for someone to blame bad things on. I told them also that Mrs. Rayes and I had registered him for first grade under the name of Humphry Cotton. I added that Humphry wanted to come meet them during spring break and that he was a little homesick to see Gunner, even though he now had Lady, his new perlino.

When I was finished, I signed it and put it in the envelope and wrote their address, with my name and the ranch address as a return address. Then I went and asked Mrs. Rayes for a stamp, which she gave me, telling me she would mail it for me if I wanted her to.

"Thank you, Mrs. Rayes. I really appreciate everything you and Mr. Rayes have done for me and Humphry," I told her.

"You're welcome, James. We loved every minute of it. Now you need to get washed up because supper is about ready," she replied.

"Yes, ma'am," I said.

When everyone was seated at the table, Mr. Rayes said grace and looked at me and commented, "It sounds like you three had quite a day in town. Hum's been telling me all about it. Says he starts school Monday. And he seems excited about it."

I smiled. I was glad Humphry was excited about going to school. He would be more excited when he began meeting new friends his age. I, too, was looking forward to his first few days of school and of hearing about the new friends he would meet.

"I'm glad he is excited about going to school," I commented. "We'll be hearing all about his teacher and his new friends."

"Do you think they will like me at school?" Humphry spoke up.

"I'm sure they will, Hum," I told him. "You don't need to worry about that."

I hadn't considered that Humphry would worry about being liked at school. With his personality, they couldn't help but like him. I guess his concern was because he had never been around kids his own age, only his brother Wayne. But knowing Humphry, it wouldn't take long for him to adjust to school life.

After supper, I told him about writing to my folks and that I had told them he wanted to meet them during the spring break.

"I know they will want to meet you too, Humphry," I told him.

HUMPHRY DID IT!

His eyes sparkled, and one of his beautiful smiles graced his face.

* * * * *

I drove Humphry to school Monday morning and walked with him to the room he was assigned with his teacher, a Mrs. Tomlin.

I introduced him to her, and she told him, "Welcome to the first grade, Humphry. I'm glad to have you. We're going to get along fine."

She was rewarded with one of his heartwarming smiles. I asked her what time I needed to be there to pick him up.

"First grade gets out at 2:15 p.m.," she told me.

I bent and gave him a hug and told him I would be there to pick him up after his class let out for the day. I explained to Mrs. Tomlin that we called him Hum out at the ranch and that if she preferred to call him that, it would be okay. She smiled and thanked me. I turned and walked away from the classroom, leaving Humphry with his teacher.

I liked Mrs. Tomlin. She was middle-aged with brown hair and soft brown eyes. She had a gentle voice and a kindly look about her face.

Mrs. Rayes asked me about her when I got back to the ranch.

She wanted to know, "Does she seem to be a good person? Does Hum like her? What time does he get out of school?"

I answered her as best I could.

That afternoon when I picked Humphry up from school, I asked him how he liked his first day at school.

"Fine!" he said, beaming all over. "I met lots of other kids, and I like the teacher too!"

I was glad for and proud of him. He would do okay in first grade.

His enthusiasm carried over to Grandma and Grandpa Rayes and to the uncles who in turn gave him a hug and told him they were proud of him too.

It was three weeks later that a letter came from Mom. She wanted to know if I would ask Mr. and Mrs. Rayes if it would be all right for her and Dad to come to the ranch for Thanksgiving.

I asked them, and they both agreed for my parents to come for the holiday.

That evening, after I had picked Humphry up from school, I worked with one of the stud colts my boss wanted broken and trained for a special equine event. My mind wasn't fully focused on what I was doing, and the stud colt managed to throw me into a fence post on the corral. The force broke the upper bone in my right arm.

Mr. Rayes caught the colt while Lyle helped me to the pickup. Mrs. Rayes came to see what was going on and immediately took charge of driving me into Miami to the hospital to get the bone in my arm taken care of.

Dr. Roberts was stern when he told me to leave the cast alone and not do anything to pull that bone apart again.

"How long will it have to be in the cast?" I ask him.

"At least three weeks," he answered. "You can come back and see me then, and we will see if it has healed enough to take the cast off. And I advise leaving the arm in a sling so you don't accidently bump into something with it and injure it worse."

"Thank you, Dr. Roberts," I said.

He looked at Mrs. Rayes and told her, "If you need anything, then call me. These pills will dull the pain for his arm. Make sure he takes them."

"I will, Doctor," she said as she put the pills in her purse.

HUMPHRY DID IT!

It was after dark before we got back to the ranch. Everyone wanted to know about my arm, and Humphry—bless his little heart—told me, "James, I'll do your chores for you!"

"No, Hum, Steve and I will do the chores James has been doing," Mr. Rayes countered. "I can't have you trying to break horses yet. Maybe in a few years, but not right now."

"But, Grandpa, I'm six now. I can help some," Humphry protested.

"I love you, Humphry, and I love it that you want to help, but, son, breaking horses is not an easy chore. A horse like the one James was working with can get you hurt, just like it did him, and maybe killed. I'd rather that didn't happen to you. Besides, your Grandma and Grandpa Cotton will be here for Thanksgiving, and I'd rather not have to tell them something happened to you. Hopefully by then, James will be able to resume his duties as a horse trainer. If not, well, the rest of us can fill in for him until James can do it," Mr. Rayes explained to the six-year-old.

Humphry looked sullen, but he said, "Okay, Grandpa."

Mr. Rayes gave him a hug.

I found things to do such as oiling the saddles and harnesses, but there's only so much a person can do. So I took over weeding the garden and bringing in whatever Mrs. Rayes wanted to fix with supper. The afternoon I saw a rattler, I went to the blacksmith shop and asked Lyle if he had a rifle handy. He asked what I needed it for, and I told him about the rattler in the garden. He didn't hesitate. He went to the bunk and took the .22 from the rack and walked with me to the garden.

I showed him the aisle the rattler was in. It was still there—all eleven feet of it. Lyle slowly lifted the rifle to his shoulder and shot the rattler. Its head went flying along the row several feet while its body writhed on the ground for a while.

"I'm glad Humphry wasn't out here," I commented.

"No kiddin'!" Lyle agreed.

He went back to get a rake to pick up the dead snake and carry it to the back of the pickup and brought back a shovel to get its head. Then he drove off to the pasture somewhere and buried it.

When he came back, he told me, "James, they say snakes travel in pairs, so its mate is apt to show up in the garden later on. You be careful out there."

I assured him I would be.

When I went inside with fresh tomatoes and carrots from the garden, Mrs. Rayes wanted to know what the shooting was about. I told her about the snake and Lyle killing it and taking it out in the pasture to bury it.

"Thank goodness little Hum wasn't out there!" she stated. "I think we better keep him away from that area for a while—at least until the mate can be found and killed."

I thought it was a good idea too.

"You know," she said thoughtfully, "that snake may have been what caused that stud colt to buck like he did. He may have sensed it near the corral."

At her reasoning, I decided I'd rather have a broken arm than die by the venom injected by a rattler. I just hoped we could find its mate before that charming six-year-old boy did. It sent chills through me just thinking about Humphry coming face to face with a snake that size.

During supper, no one mentioned the snake. If Humphry didn't know about it, he wouldn't have a reason to be curious and go looking to find the mate.

Bob asked me if I wanted to go with him the next morning. He and Andy were going to check the fences and check the ponds and the windmills. I accepted his offer. It had been a while since I had been able to ride with them for any reason.

Mr. Rayes had assigned the horses over to Steve to break and train. Steve was just as good as I am at that—maybe better at some. Lady was already trained enough for Humphry to ride, so he didn't have to deal with her.

After Humphry was in bed and asleep, Mr. Rayes came to the bunkhouse and talked with us menfolk, telling us to carry rifles and keep an eye out for the mate to the rattler Lyle had killed, and if we came across the den or the snake to let him know. We would kill the snake and let him know if we found a den of baby snakes so he could pour gasoline into the den. He made all of us promise not to talk about snakes around the boy.

"If he comes to you and tells you he saw one, make him show you where. Then you can kill it and talk to him about them. Otherwise, keep it under your hats," Mr. Rayes reminded.

Bob, who was usually quiet, spoke, "Mr. Rayes, in case you hadn't noticed, we're all grown men. We know what to talk about and when to talk about it to the boy. And another thing, we all love that boy too. In fact, we've come to realize that we need him as much as he needs all of us. So the quickest way to lose your entire crew is to let something happen to Hum."

Mr. Rayes was caught by surprise, as were the rest of us.

He looked puzzled at Bob and asked him, "Were you thinking of quitting Bob?"

"Nope, but if anything happens to Hum, you stand to lose us all. I just wanted you to know. James told us how he came by the boy. Personally, I think God sent James to him. He's a good boy. He doesn't bother anything unless he asks about it first. He's willing to do anything he can to help out. He has tried to put his former life behind him and build a new life. We have all become his new family. And if we can help it at all, we're not going to let anything happen to him."

Mr. Rayes grinned. "Okay, Bob. I didn't realize you men felt that way about Hum. Now that I know, I won't have to worry about him being taken care of."

He turned and walked out the door.

I thanked Bob for what he'd said about Humphry. I hadn't heard Bob talk that much for some time. He was the oldest among us and had been with Rayes longer than any of us. He had been working with the rest of us long enough to know all of us inside out.

"Bob, what do you tell folks in town when they get snooty and tell you they didn't know I have a son? Do they ask you where his mother is?" I asked him. "I know you've heard those things said and asked."

"I tell them the truth, James. You came here to find a job, and afterward, the wife refused to move down here. But after she died, you went and got your son. When they want to know how she died,

I tell them she died in a house fire and that Hum managed to get out of the house but she didn't. From what you told us, that's the way of it. And it's nobody's business that you were never married to Hum's mother," Bob told me.

"Thanks, Bob. I appreciate that. You've just given me the answers to those questions. I wasn't real sure how to respond to them," I said.

"You know, I'm not too much of a religious man, James. But I do feel God sent you by the Hargrove place and that He brought you back by it to retrieve Humphry and give him a decent home. And I think God will forgive me of one little lie about you being married to the woman."

He put a hand on my shoulder and gave it a squeeze. Then he turned and went to his bunk.

Now it was Steve's turn to talk.

"You know, James, me and Bob and Lyle don't have any family anywhere left alive. Andy only has a brother somewhere that he hasn't seen in a lot of years. So we can appreciate Hum not having any family. And when he started calling all of us uncle, it gave us a reason to think of him as a nephew, and we have since become family to him and him to us. We have slowly come to realize we all needed to be family. Maybe we have all grown up since living around Hum."

"One thing about him," Andy put in, "is that he pays attention to what he's being taught. And he doesn't act up or try to be smart aleck like some kids do."

"And he's smart," Lyle said. "Maybe a little too mature for his age. But he retains what he learns. With some kids, things go in one ear and out the other. But not with Hum. He can do something one time, and from then on it's his."

"Thanks, guys," I told them.

It was comforting to know how the men all felt about Hum.

I had been concerned that I might have to find a babysitter for him. In a sense, I guess I did. I doubt I could have found a babysitter who would have been as good to him as were his "uncles" here at the Slant T.

The next morning, I rode with Bob and Andy, checking the fence lines and the water holes and windmills. We cleaned out two of the water holes, stapled wires back to posts where the deer had crossed and pulled them loose, and we found one windmill in need of repair. According to Bob, it needed the leathers replaced. I didn't know anything about that, and Andy had never done it, although he knew how to oil the wheel at the top of it—something else I didn't know. I had never had to fool with the windmills in all the time I had worked at the Slant T.

"We will have to make a trip to town to get what we need to fix this windmill. Tomorrow, you can both help me fix this one," Bob informed us.

Andy and I both nodded.

The rest of the day went well. The cattle all looked good. Some of them looked up as we rode by them and went back to grazing. The horses, too, gave us a once-over and resumed eating. A couple of them gave us a neighing greeting and moved over a few feet. They looked good. I let my gaze run over them, wondering which of them would be next in the training corral.

We were halfway back to the ranch houses when we ran across the mate to the rattler Lyle had killed a few days ago. Andy's horse snorted and put both ears forward and refused to go forward any further. We didn't see the snake at first, but the horse knew it was there.

Bob spotted it first crawling through a maze of small rocks just ahead of us. He drew his rifle up to his shoulder, and when it showed itself where he could get a good shot, he shot it. We left it lay for the buzzards to feast on. We told Mr. Rayes about it when we got back to the ranch, and Bob told him he needed to go to town and pick up the things he needed to pull the windmill and fix it.

Humphry came out to greet us as we rode into the corral. He gave each of us a hug, then began excitedly telling us about his day at school, which brought smiles from all of us. Mrs. Tomlin had brought cookies for them and brought some small containers of milk for the class. Half an hour before time for class to let out, she let them eat cookies and drink their milk.

"I take it you like Mrs. Tomlin," I said.

"Yeah! She's great. And I like Rory and Tony too. They both live on ranches like us," he replied.

"Maybe we can meet them one of these days," Mr. Rayes commented. "Do you happen to know their last names? I may know their fathers."

"Yeah, Grandpa. Rory's last name is Peters, and Tony's is Matthews." Hum answered.

Mr. Rayes nodded and said to no one in particular, "Circle P and Three Bar M."

"You know them, Grandpa?"

"Yes," Mr. Rayes said. "Morris Peters has a ranch on the east side of Miami, and Tracy Matthews has one on the south side of Miami. Both big ranchers and cattlemen."

He looked thoughtful for a few minutes, then suggested that he could sponsor a holiday party and invite them and other ranchers to come to it so Hum could meet them.

"How about a Halloween party, Grandpa?" Humphry asked.

Grant Rayes rubbed his chin then looked thoughtfully at Humphry.

"You know, Humphry," he said at last, "that just sounds like a wonderful idea. We could have a barbeque, an egg hunt, an apple dunk, candy for the kids, a tub of beer, and a tub of sodas. How does that sound?"

"It would sound better with a band and a dance," Lyle told him. "That way, Hum can show off his talent too."

"Uncle Lyle!" Humphry exclaimed.

Lyle reached over and rumpled Humphry's hair.

"No need to be scared, Hum. Your Uncle Lyle will be there too."

* * * * *

The next few weeks were spent partially in preparation of the Halloween celebration on the Slant T. An area was leveled for folks to park their buggies. Extra hitching rails were set up for extra riders to which to tie their mounts. A large pit was dug and prepared for barbequing the side of beef Rayes had ordered. The extra side was hung in the smokehouse.

Humphry was given the task to cut small squares of paper and numbering them from one to one hundred. The numbers were put into a large jar and shaken for the drawing for the extra side of beef. He was also given the chore of helping color six dozen eggs for the egg hunt with witches and pumpkins and black cats. And he made some of the Halloween decorations for the outside event. They ranged from scarecrows to black cats and witches and cardboard pumpkins with delightful faces.

Invitations were sent out, including one to the teacher. The day of the celebration Mr. Rayes and Bob ran a metal rod through the side of beef and mounted it on the spit. They lit the grilling bricks under it and started cooking it early that morning to get it done in time for the guests as they arrived. I volunteered for the first hour of turning the side of beef. My arm was still in the cast, so I wouldn't be much good for doing anything else, I figured. Besides, it kept me out of the way of everyone else.

Mrs. Rayes made her own barbeque for spreading across the carcass. She had busied herself with baking apple pies and cupcakes for the event. She had also put together a large bowl of potato salad from the potatoes out of her garden.

Toward noon, the guests began arriving. First were the Donnahues from just east of the Slant T, Brennans were next, then the banker, followed by the Peters family, and a multitude of others, including the Matthews family. There must have been at least sixty or seventy people who came. And to Humphry's delight, his friends Rory and Tony, his classmates, also came.

Humphrey showed his friends his perlino mare, Lady. He had brushed and combed Lady to perfection. Her coat glistened. She snickered a soft welcome to Rory and Tony as they began petting her.

"Gee whiz, Humphrey, she's pretty!" Tony exclaimed.

"Do you ride her a lot?" Rory asked.

"I ride her some, but not every day," Humphrey replied. "I picked her out all by myself. Grandpa took me out to the horses and let me look them over."

"How come you chose her?" Tony asked him.

"I liked her, and I like her color," Humphrey explained. "And James broke her and trained her for me to ride. He's good with horses. I hope someday I can be as good as he and Uncle Steve are."

"What else do you have to do around here?" Rory asked.

"I don't have to do anything, but I gather the eggs for Grandma Rayes and feed and water the chickens. In the evenings, I help James weed and water the garden. Grandma has a big garden, and I like being out there," Humphrey told his friends.

Tony's mother called him. Humphrey and Rory walked back to the house with him.

Mrs. Rayes was handing paper bags to the children. It was time for the egg hunt. She told each child they could keep the eggs they found, if they wanted to. They scattered to find their treasures. When they had found all the eggs, it was time to eat. And after enjoying a healthy meal, Mrs. Rayes let each child pick a caramel-covered apple to eat. She also let them choose a bag of Halloween candy into which she had added little keepsake trinkets. She had rolled down the tops of the bags so the children couldn't cheat by looking into the bags to see which bag they wanted.

When she was through with that Mr. Rayes told the audience, "Friends and fellow neighbors, I have a surprise for you. Lyle and Humphrey, bring your guitars and come up here."

He had Lyle and Humphrey stand on the porch to play and sing to the crowd before them.

They only sang four songs because that was all Humphrey had learned so far. The visitors loved it. Some of them knew Lyle could play a guitar, but none of them—not even Tony and Rory—knew that Humphrey was learning to play one.

HUMPHRY DID IT!

I was proud of them. As a duet, they were a sensation. If Humphry was nervous at all, he didn't show it. He played and sang like he had been doing it all of his life. He and Lyle both received lots of compliments for their performance.

Mr. Matthews told Grant Rayes, "You've been holding out on us, Rayes!"

The boss nodded toward Humphry and asked him, "What do you think of my boy?"

"From what I've seen of him and heard of him from Tony, I think he's mighty fine boy," Mr. Matthews answered. "I understand he and Tony pal around with Rory Peters at school. I would be willing to bet those three grow up to best friends."

19

Autumn had started turning on her parade of color, turning the leaves of the trees from green to orange and yellow and brown colors. They were pretty, but they were a bleak reminder that winter was on the way. The wind took on a light chill that became more chilling as the weeks passed.

The ranch was a hustle of cowboys trying to get the prairie hay mowed, baled, and brought into to the barn loft for winter storage where it would be out of the weather for feeding the cattle and horses closest to the home spread.

Humphry kept his grades up at school. On mornings, he still gathered eggs and fed and watered the chickens. After the Halloween party, Mr. Rayes chose the following weekend for Humphry to clean out the chicken house. He gave the boy instructions as to what he wanted him to do and how he wanted it done and told Hum to take his time with it.

Humphry did, and he did a good job of cleaning the chicken house. When he came to ask Mr. Rayes if he wanted to come check it, the boss was surprised at how well Humphry had done.

"Hum, you have done a really good job! Now let me help you put in fresh straw for the hens. We'll put some in their nests and cover the floor to help them stay warmer this winter," he said.

Humphry followed Mr. Rayes to where the straw was stacked and helped bring straw back to the henhouse. Some of the chickens clucked at them as if to ask them what they were doing, which made Humphry laugh.

"Grandma should have nice, clean eggs in the morning!" Humphry said cheerfully.

"Yeah, I guess so," Mr. Rayes grinned.

After a moment he asked, "Hum, are you excited about meeting your Grandma and Grandpa Cotton?"

"I guess so," Humphry answered. "I hope they're as nice as James is."

"I'm sure they will be," Mr. Rayes assured him. "You think a lot of James, don't you?"

"Yeah," Hum told him, looking up at him. "James is my friend. And he told me it's okay if I call him James even though that judge gave him custody of me. I don't tell that to the kids at school. And if they ask about my mama, I just tell them she died. And they don't ask me anything else."

"You're a smart boy," Mr. Rayes told him.

They stepped inside the house where Mrs. Rayes had just pulled a large roast from the oven. The aroma met them just inside the door.

Looking behind her, Mrs. Rayes asked, "Can I get you guys to go out to the garden and see if you can dig me up some nice potatoes to go with supper?"

"Sure, Grandma. Me and Grandpa will go get them for you. You want some onions too?" Humphry asked.

"You might bring in a couple," she said smiling, handing him the basket she used for that purpose.

Mr. Rayes grinned and shook his head and followed the youngster out the door toward the garden. He stopped to get the shovel from the toolshed before following Humphry to the potato row.

The ground was hard, but it didn't take long with Mr. Rayes manning the shovel and Humphry picking the potatoes, brushing them off and putting them into the basket for them to fill it. Moving over to the onions, Mr. Rayes again applied the shovel and turned up some nice-sized onions.

"Hum," he said, "I think we better turn on the water for a while and give these veggies a drink."

"I'll do it!" Humphry volunteered.

Mr. Rayes put the shovel back in the toolshed and waited for Humphry to catch up with him. They walked back to the house and gave Mrs. Rayes the vegetables she was going to use to go with the roast.

"Will we have enough potatoes to have some for Thanksgiving dinner?" Mrs. Rayes asked her husband.

Thanksgiving was still twelve days away, but she wanted to be sure she had enough of everything to go around. She had already planned most of what they would have for the Thanksgiving dinner. There were still enough ears of corn in the garden that she could fix some of those, and she had planned on Grant shooting a wild turkey for it. She would make gravy from the drippings from it to go over the potatoes and homemade dressing. She planned on baking homemade dinner rolls to go with dinner, and pies would be on hand for dessert.

"Yes, honey, I think we have plenty of potatoes left and plenty of corn too. Onions, if you need them. And probably enough carrots," he told her.

Humphry took off his coat and went to his room. He checked to make sure everything was in place and that he hadn't left any dirty clothes lying around anywhere. He wanted his room to look nice when James's parents got there. In fact, he wanted to impress them so they would like him. He was anxious to meet them.

He picked up his guitar and began to play it, and without realizing it he began to sing the songs Uncle Lyle had taught him. Then he remembered that Uncle Lyle was teaching him yet another song. So he took his guitar, stopped to put on his coat, and told the Mr. and Mrs. Rayes that he was going to the bunkhouse to practice with Uncle Lyle.

"You know, Grant, he's going to be a good singer when he gets a little older," Mrs. Rayes commented.

Her husband agreed, saying, "He already does a pretty fair job of it."

* * * * *

Lyle was playing a hand of poker with Bob and Steve. Humphry stood silently watching them. When the hand was over, Lyle quit and got his guitar.

He and Humphry moved away from the table, and Lyle asked, "Do you remember where we were on the last song you were learning?"

Humphry nodded and began to play it. He played to where he had stopped last time, and Lyle showed him where to place his fingers on the frets to continue. It took a few minutes, but Hum finally had the hang of it. They played a duet of the song then. Steve and Bob listened patiently to their young companion and their coworker.

Andy and I walked in on all of them singing "The Red River Valley." Steve and Bob were a little rusty, but over all, they did a good job. Lyle invited me and Andy to join in, and we did.

Andy began clapping his hands together with the rhythm of the music. All of us were having a good time. None of us could have said how long our boss and his wife had stood in the doorway listening to us carry on.

At the end of one song, Mr. Rayes told us, "Mom threatened to throw supper out if it got cold. So you fellers might ought to come eat."

We all rose. Lyle put his guitar back where he kept it, and Humphry carried his with him to the house.

"You guys were pretty good," Mrs. Rayes told us as we walked up to the main house. "I might just make you sing for your supper every night."

Lyle swallowed that hook, line, and sinker and replied, "That would be a good idea. That way, Hum here could practice for when his other grandparents get here."

The rest of us hired hands could have throttled him, but we knew he meant well. There were only twelve more days to Thanksgiving Day, and I knew my parents would be thrilled to listen to Humphry. I felt sure Mr. Rayes also thought about the rest of us giving a performance.

In a couple of days, my arm would be out of the cast and maybe I could handle more of the chores. But that didn't do anything for my singing ability. I was fairly sure someone—maybe Mom—would want to hear a duet with just me and Humphry while she and Dad were here.

20

Mrs. Rayes drove me to the doctor to get my cast cut from my arm. The doctor's advice was to be careful with it for the next couple of weeks and not to do any heavy lifting for a while. I thanked him and paid him before we left his office.

"It's a good thing I came with you, James. I can tell Grant what the doctor said about your arm. He will believe me where he might not have believed you," she told me.

I couldn't argue with her. There had been times when I had felt Mr. Rayes didn't want to completely believe me on things I told him. It was always good to have someone around who could back me up when those times happened.

Mrs. Rayes stopped at the grocery store to pick up a few things she needed. I found Humphry some of the peppermint sticks he enjoyed and endured her protest while I paid for the things she had picked out.

We stopped by the filling station, and I filled the pickup. It was just under a half a tank, but I wanted it full for the holidays—as Dad had always said—just in case. He also told me it was just as easy to keep the top half full as the bottom half, and then if you should have an emergency, you had a full tank of gas to go to wherever you needed to go.

"When are your parents supposed to be here, James?" Mrs. Rayes asked.

"They'll be here the day before Thanksgiving. I think that's the twenty-seventh. It will probably be sometime in the afternoon before they get here. And Mom said they would get a room in one of the motels in town," I answered her. "I think you'll like Mom. She's a lot like you, and like you, she's a good cook."

"I can hardly wait for them to get here," she said.

I knew the feeling. I, too, was anxious for them to get here. And I wanted to talk to Dad as to what he thought about me going ahead and adopting little Humphry and having his last name legally changed to Cotton. He was going by it anyway at school, but later, as he would get older, that might pose some complications, unless I could have it legally changed to Cotton. In a few years he would need a Social Security card, and it needed to be in his legal name. Later, he would need it for a driver's license also.

With those thoughts in mind, I talked to Humphry that evening. I wanted to know what he thought about being legally Humphry Cotton rather than Humphry Hargrove.

He threw his arms around my neck and exclaimed, "I'd love to be Humphry Cotton, James!"

He gave me one of those beautiful, heart-grabbing smiles, and I swear his whole body lit up. I couldn't have made him any happier. His reply couldn't have made me any happier either.

Later, I expressed to Mr. and Mrs. Rayes about wanting to adopt Humphry and have his name changed to mine. They both nodded in agreement and said they thought it was a good idea. I told them I wanted to talk to my folks after they meet Humphry and see what they think of it.

"I'll bet they will be thrilled about it," Mrs. Rayes commented. "After all, they don't have any grandchildren right now. And they can't help but love Humphry."

Mr. Rayes twinkled, and with a smile, he said, "Maybe one of these days there'll be a young Mrs. Cotton around to help you raise him."

I told him I hadn't found any one who qualified for that.

Still smiling, he told me, "You will one day."

I returned his smile, but mentally, I was thinking it would take a very special person to qualify as Humphry's stepmother—someone gentle, someone caring, someone who would love him for himself, and not someone jealous enough to blame things on Humphry with that echo from his past of "Humphry did it!" It would take me meeting women too. Here on the Slant T, I rarely ever saw a woman other than occasionally when the boss or his wife needed me to go to town for something. And even though we went to church on Sundays, so far, I hadn't seen any young women who would fill the bill for the woman I thought I wanted for Humphry as a stepmother—or whom I wanted to be around, for that matter.

Two days before Thanksgiving, Mr. Rayes took Andy with him to hunt some wild turkeys. They were gone most of the day. The sun was beginning to set by the time they got back to the ranch. They had found turkeys. They each held up one to show the rest of us. This year, the turkeys were bigger than usual. They must have weighed at least twenty-five to thirty pounds apiece.

Bob fetched a large washtub while Steve and I put together a fire to boil water in. After the turkeys were scalded to the point we could pluck their feathers from their bodies, Lyle and Mr. Rayes found a tree and some short ropes and hung the turkeys to tree limbs by tying short pieces of cotton rope around their legs. Once plucked, the men plunged the turkeys into the still-hot water once more to make sure they had gotten all the small feathers. Then he took them to the log we normally chopped wood on and used the ax—this time, to sever the heads of the turkeys from their bodies.

He had the boys add some cold water to the tub to cool it down some and commenced to cut one turkey open and remove the entrails, careful to cut the liver, gizzard, and heart from them. He did the second one the same way. Mr. Rayes then carried both turkeys to the house and came back with a small bowl into which he put the livers, gizzards, and hearts and took those back to the house.

When he came back this time, he had us carry the tub out to the garden and empty the water down a row of vegetables. The rest of the intestines he put into a plastic bucket with a lid to bury somewhere in the pasture the nest morning. We cleaned up the mess we had made in the yard, including the place we had built the fire to heat the tub of water.

Mrs. Rayes removed the feet portions of the legs and also the necks and wrapped them with a liver, a heart, and a gizzard then put one package of each inside the two turkeys. She froze the smaller turkey, and the other she refrigerated to keep it cool until she was ready to put it in the oven for the Thanksgiving Day dinner. That was because my parents would be here tomorrow, and Mrs. Rayes allowed for that in electing to bake the larger turkey.

My parents showed up shortly after three in the afternoon. I shook hands with Dad and gave Mom a hug. Then I introduced Humphry to them.

"Hi, Humphry. We've heard a lot about you from James," Dad said.

"He's cute! James, you've been holding out on us!" Mom declared.

Humphry produced one of his beautiful smiles as he told them both, "Hi."

"Come on up to the house and meet Mr. and Mrs. Rayes," I invited.

As we started forward, the boss and his wife came outside to greet us. I introduced Mom and Dad to them. Grant shook hands with Dad, telling him it was good to finally get to meet him.

Mrs. Rayes did the same with Mom, telling her, "I'm so glad you could come and spend Thanksgiving with us. James has told us so much about you, and I have been anxious to meet you, and so has Grant. Come on inside."

As they entered the house, Mr. Rayes and Dad fell into talking about cattle, hay, weather, and other ranch-related topics.

Mom asked Mrs. Rayes if there was anything she could do to help her in the kitchen.

Mrs. Rayes told her no then, turning to Humphry, asked him, "Hum, why don't you show your Grandma Cotton your room?"

"Okay," Humphry said, heading down the hallway to his room, with Mom following him.

He showed her his school projects first, and Mom asked, "Do you like school, Humphry?"

"Yeah I do, and I like most of the other kids, but Rory and Tony are my friends," he answered.

"That's wonderful, Humphry," Mom commented. "Does James stay up here in the main house too?"

"No, ma'am, he lives in the bunkhouse with Uncle Lyle and Uncle Andy and Uncle Bob and Uncle Steve. You will get to meet them at suppertime 'cause they eat in the house with us," he replied.

"You can call me Grandma Cotton, if you want to," she told him.

That brought another wonderful smile.

Humphry hugged her and told her, "Okay."

Mom noticed his guitar and asked him if he could play it, and he explained that Uncle Lyle was teaching him to play it.

"That's good. Maybe before Grandpa Cotton and I have to leave we can listen to you play a song or two," she said.

Humphry smiled and said nothing. Mom decided she and Humphry should join everyone else.

I volunteered to go to the bunkhouse and let the rest of the hired hands know supper was almost ready. I wasn't surprised that they had all cleaned up and put on presentable clothes. I walked back to the house with them and introduced them to Mom and Dad. Dad shook hands with each of them in turn, and he and Mom both told them they were pleased to meet them.

After supper, while Mom helped Mrs. Rayes with clearing the kitchen, the rest of us retired to the living room; and when Mom and Mrs. Rayes joined us, he told Dad he had a surprise for him and Mom. He sent Lyle and Humphry to get their guitars, then asked them to sing a few songs for us. Mom and Dad were delighted, and they enjoyed the presentation as much if not more than the rest of us.

Dad told Humphry and Lyle they had done a good job of picking and singing.

"Humphry is quick to learn and learn how to play his guitar," Lyle said. "And he has a good singing voice for one so young. I expect in a few years he may be playing in public or at least in the school festivities."

"Probably so," Dad agreed.

Humphry was beaming and proud his new grandparents had enjoyed listening to him and Uncle Lyle perform for them.

"He's getting pretty good with the horses too," Mr. Rayes put in. "One of these days, he'll be as good as James and Steve are. Maybe tomorrow he can show you his mare. I took him with me one day right after James brought him home and let him pick out the horse he wanted. He chose a nice little perlino mare that James broke for him to ride."

"I'd love to see your horse, Humphry," Dad told the youngster.

Humphry's pride rose a few degrees, and he said, "I'll show you to her tomorrow morning, Grandpa Cotton. Her name is Lady, and I love her. I miss Gunner, but I love Lady."

"I think Gunner misses you and James too. He's a good stallion, and he's doing all right. Maybe James can bring you out to visit at our house after school lets out," Dad responded.

I hadn't thought about Humphry missing Gunner. I knew the day I let him ride Gunner on the way back to his house from the pasture where Mr. Sweney and I had fixed the fence was a memory he would treasure. But until now, I hadn't realized how much of a memory it was for the boy.

Mom and Dad had a motel room in town, and at length, they elected to leave, saying they would be back in the morning.

21

Thanksgiving Day dawned with bright skies and pleasant weather. Mom had brought along a quart jar of her homemade cranberry sauce and two deep-dish apple pies to go along with the dinner Mrs. Rayes put on the table.

We men went to the bunkhouse while the women were preparing the food for Thanksgiving dinner. Dad and Mr. Rayes caught up on the local cattlemen news and produce, and the rest of us just listened, including Humphry.

Dad asked Mr. Rayes if he had ordered the new Canadian wheat, and Mr. Rayes told him no.

"But if you'll let me know how it does for you, I may consider it for next winter," he told Dad.

Dad agreed.

I was happy Dad and Mr. Rayes got along so well.

Humphry finally could stand it no longer.

"Grandpa Cotton, would you like to see my mare, Lady?" he asked Dad.

"Why, yes, Humphry, I would," Dad answered.

"She's in the barn. I had Hum put her in a stall because some of the hunters shoot at anything, and they don't stop to see what it is before they shoot it. I didn't want Lady to be shot by some mindless hunter," Mr. Rayes explained.

"Come on," Humphry told them as he proudly led the way to the barn where his mare was housed in a large stall.

They stopped at the stall, and Humphry told the mare, "Lady, this is Grandpa Cotton. You already know Grandpa Rayes."

HUMPHRY DID IT!

The mare snickered a welcome, and Dad reached an arm out and began to pet her.

"She's nice," Dad said. "And pretty too. I see why you put her in the barn during the holidays. And I know why Humphry picked her over the other horses. Perlinos are smart horses, and usually, if they are with other horses, they become the lead mare."

"I wasn't aware of that, but James gentled her down and trained her for Hum. She isn't trained to work cattle yet, but she is trained enough so Hum can ride her anywhere," Mr. Rayes told my Dad.

Dad nodded. "That stallion he rode home is certainly nice. He's easy to ride too."

"Usually by the time James and Steve get through with them, they are pretty well trained," Mr. Rayes commented.

"Give the devil his due," I said. "There are some things about training that Steve is better at than I am."

Mr. Rayes smiled and told me, "Well, between the two of you, I get some well-broke horses."

"Thanks," I said. "Dad, what would you say to me adopting Humphry?"

Dad took on a seriously thoughtful expression, and it was a few minutes before he spoke.

He looked at Humphry, who pulled up one of his beautiful smiles, and he looked at me.

"I think if that's what you want to do and what Humphry wants, you should look into it," Dad told me. "Bear in mind though that the boy still has a brother running loose, that even though you have custody of Humphry, the brother could feasibly block the adoption. But the judge who granted you custody of him might be able to pull a few strings for you, especially with me and Grant Rayes backing you on it."

The boss nodded and told Dad, "I told him basically the same thing. He loves the boy, and Hum loves him. I see no reason why he shouldn't adopt him. All of us here at the ranch love Humphry. You and your wife will too, once you get to really know him."

"Then I could be a Cotton!" Humphry exclaimed excitedly.

His eyes sparkled, and he still wore that heart-grabbing smile. I think he surprised Mr. Rayes as much as he did Dad and me.

Dad put an arm around Humphry's shoulders, smiled down at him, and agreed, "Yes, then you can be a Cotton."

"I'll look into it when school is out next spring," I said.

"You shouldn't have any problem," Dad told me. "But the judge may have to set a time frame for it to go to a hearing in order to find his brother—if he isn't already in jail by then—and that could take sixty to ninety days. Maybe longer. But I think in the end, he would grant the adoption. Just keep us posted when you start the proceedings. Mom and I will help you any way we can, and I'm sure Grant and his wife feel the same way."

"Yes we do," Mr. Rayes said.

I was grateful to them all, and I wished at that minute that Mom and Dad lived closer to the Slant T ranch.

Bob came into the barn and walked over to us.

"If I can borrow the button," he said, "he and I can get some feed out for the colts in the corral."

"Excuse me, Grandpas. I need to go with Uncle Bob to help feed the colts!" Humphry's happy voice told us.

He turned and hurried after Bob, leaving the rest of us smiling after him.

"For what he's been through, he's a great kid," I commented.

I told Dad about Humphry's mother scolding him for talking to strangers and how he had come back at her with "He's not a stranger. He's James. And he's my friend." I went on to tell him how rude and contemptuous Mrs. Hargrove had been, adding that she could scald embarrassment off the word *sarcasm*. Then I told him how Humphry's brother, who is nine years older than Humphry, got up in the mornings and left the house and often didn't come back until well after dark, which left Humphry to do all the chores—some of which he wasn't big enough to do but tried to do anyway. I told him how Wayne blamed Humphry for the things Wayne himself did by telling his Mom that "Humphry did it," until she caught him in a lie over the peppermint candy.

"She told him then that she wasn't putting up with any more of his shenanigans, and she laid the law down to him. I left to go on out to Guymon, and when I came back, I found the house burned and finally found Humphry in the hay loft in the barn. He told me how his brother had hit his mother and she fell into the table, knocking the lamp off. It broke and caught the house of fire, and his brother wouldn't let Humphry go back inside the house to try to get their mother out. He had shoved Humphry back into the yard. After that, Wayne had hitched the mare, Rosebud, to the trailer and left, refusing to let Humphry go with him.

"I took Humphry with me and got him cleaned up and bought him a fresh set of clothes. And then I stopped by the courthouse in Buffalo and talked to the judge, who then gave me custody of Humphry and had an all-points bulletin issued for Wayne."

Dad and Mr. Rayes exchanged looks. Both shook their heads.

"Sounds like the kid had a tough life before you came along," Dad commented.

"We don't talk about his past since he came here. He has a lot of torment to overcome, and so far, he has done a supergood job of it. He has adopted Mr. and Mrs. Rayes as his grandparents and all of the hired hands as his Uncles, and they have all graciously allowed him to do that and allowed themselves to become his family," I told Dad.

"And he takes an interest in everything, and he learns fast and helps as best he can without getting in the way. Plus, unlike other kids his age, he doesn't just pick up things, he asks if he can look at them or use them," Mr. Rayes added.

"That's good," Dad commented and then suggested that we all go back to the house.

As we stepped inside, Mrs. Rayes told us, "I was just about ready to throw all of this out to the chickens!"

She was teasing, of course, for her eyes twinkled and she donned a friendly smile.

I stepped back outside and rang the dinner triangle to summon the rest of them, then retraced my steps. Whatever the womenfolk had cooked, it smelled super delicious! I don't think I'd ever seen that much food on the table at one time. And beyond it were an assortment of desserts.

As soon as each of us were seated around the table, Dad said grace, and afterward Mr. Rayes began passing food around the table. It was great to have all my family together—my parents, Mr. and Mrs. Rayes, Humphry, and the rest of the hired hands.

I think we all stuffed ourselves to capacity and beyond. The wild turkey had a taste all its own, different from the store-bought turkeys and, to my way of thinking, much better. I liked the homemade dressing much better than the boxed mixes from the stores too. If I could have my way, Mom and Mrs. Rayes would get to cook every meal for us. You just haven't eaten until you sit down to a meal those two ladies can put before you.

I offered to help clean up the kitchen but was told that I'd just be in the way. So I went with the rest of the men to the bunkhouse where Dad had a chance to visit with Andy, Bob, Lyle, and Steve.

Since we don't often get a chance to just sit and visit and air our backgrounds, I sat and listened while the rest of the hired hands filled Dad in on the places where they had grown up, the things they had done with their lives, and how they had ended up on the Slant T ranch working for Grant Rayes.

Bob had wandered in first after losing his family to raiders who also burned him out and left him for the bank to foreclose on a few months later. Bob rarely talked to anyone about his past before the Slant T. But he opened up for Dad, and I think some of what he told Dad were things that even Mr. Rayes had not known. But Dad has that effect on people. They open up to Dad with things other people couldn't pry out of them with a crowbar.

Andy had drifted in fresh out of high school looking for a job to support himself. He was quiet and likeable and a good worker. Andy was the kind of person who spoke when he had something to say, like when he suggested we register Humphry in school with my last name since most folks around here didn't know the difference anyway.

Lyle had played with a band for several years before he got tired of constantly being on the move to play their engagements. Or, as he laughingly put it, "until the new wore off." Lyle has a good voice and plays a mean guitar. But a person would never guess it if you watched how gentle and how patient he is in teaching young Humphry to play his guitar and sing the songs that go with the music.

Steve was like me in that we both had heard the reputation of the Slant T ranch near Miami, Oklahoma. According to gossip, it was the best ranch around and the best place to work. Neither of us were looking for work at the time, but once we set foot on the Slant

T, we became a part of it. Both of us are good with training horses, and while we both are better with some of it, we work together, getting the horses broken and trained for Mr. Rayes. And when he sells them, they can be used for anything the buyer wants to use them for.

Gunner had been trained the same way. We worked with Lady when we had time to teach her to do whatever Humphry would need her for as he and the mare grew older. For now, she was where he could ride her anywhere he wanted to and be safe with her.

Later that evening when Mom and Dad left, Dad shook hands all around and gave Humphry and me both a hug. Mom gave us each a hug too. Mr. and Mrs. Rayes welcomed them back anytime they felt like coming.

22

December came in with the usual snow and biting-cold wind making it miserable to be outdoors. Humphry still tended the chickens in the mornings and brought in the eggs. The chickens themselves hurried to eat their food and went back into the chicken coop out of the cold.

We fed the livestock and made sure the ponds and tanks were clear of ice so they could drink. But then, one stormy night brought in a blizzard, and the cattle hunkered in the corners of the fences and were determined to stay there. We had difficulty getting them to move so they wouldn't stand there and freeze to death. The horses we rode weren't too happy about having to work in that kind of weather, but we managed to get the cattle into a more sheltered area and fed them there.

The horse herd sought shelter too, and we fed them where they were, knowing the stallion would make them exercise. And the horses had sense enough to rotate positions to keep themselves reasonably warm, usually with the youngest foals to the inner circle of where they were. And the mares had sense enough to pull some of the hay down to make bedding for the young ones, even covering the foals with the hay if the weather got bad enough. At times, they gathered inside the shelters Mr. Rayes had built but not always.

On the weekends, young Humphry rode with us in the pickup or truck, but we made him stay inside the cab most of the time. He always asked if he could get out of the vehicle or if he could help us do something. Usually there wasn't anything we dared let him do besides watch from inside the vehicle, especially on days when the snow was coming down. Even so, he enjoyed going with us and watching us feed the livestock.

Once in a while, Mr. Rayes would allow him to shovel snow from the main house to make the paths leading to the chicken house and the barn and bunkhouse. Mrs. Rayes always had hot chocolate ready for him to drink when he came into the house from shoveling snow. Sometimes, there was enough of it for us older guys too, and I think we enjoyed it as much as Humphry did.

Two days before Christmas, the snow drifted and froze on top of the drifts, allowing the animals we kept in the corral near the barn to walk on top of the drifts and wander off. It took us most of the day to find them and bring them back to the barn where we left the top half of the door latched back so they could get air. We then shoveled the snowdrift down to the ground level in the corral. By the time we finished, it was beginning to grow dark, and all of us were ready to get in out of the cold.

We had set up a live Christmas tree, and it held on to handmade memories between the rows of Christmas tree lights. We hands had gone together, just as we always had to get gifts for Mr. and Mrs. Rayes. We had drawn names for a gift to get for the name we drew of us hands. But everyone went all out it seemed to get gifts for Humphry and to make sure the youngster had the best Christmas ever. Humphry too had made some handmade gifts for everyone. I don't know when he made them or how he managed to keep any of us from knowing about it. But he managed.

We were all surprised, and Humphry glowed! He was as happy about us receiving his gifts as he was receiving ours. Mom and Dad had sent presents for Humphry too, and he was thrilled about getting gifts from Grandma and Grandpa Cotton too. This was a Christmas he was going to remember above and beyond the ones he would share in his future. It was more special than any other would ever be because it was the first one that let him know what Christmas is all about and because it was shared with people who loved him and shared with folks who would never blame him for things he hadn't done and from whom he would never hear a negative "Humphry did it!"

Each of us in turn told him, "Thank you, Humphry!" and we sincerely meant it.

Christmas dinner was another great meal that Mrs. Rayes had fixed for us. By the time we finished eating, I don't think any of us had room for another bite. That probably was a good thing because just as we got up from the table, it began to snow. We had to hurry to get from the main house to the bunkhouse before it really began coming down.

I offered to help Mrs. Rayes clean the kitchen, but Mr. Rayes told me, "Never mind, James. I'll help her with the kitchen. And I expect Humphry had better stay here. He doesn't need to catch cold from being out in this weather."

I gave Humphry a hug and told him I am proud of him.

"Be a good boy, Humphry," I told him. "I love you. Good night."

He hugged me back and said, "I love you too, James."

The boss and his wife were both smiling as I went out the door. I figured young Humphry was in for some more spoiling before bedtime. It would do him good.

* * * * *

School started back on the third of January. It was a blustery, cold day, but at least it wasn't snowing. All the youngsters seemed to be happy to be back at school—or, I thought to myself, glad to be back with their friends and able to exchange visitations about their Christmas Day and their new gifts. I watched for a few minutes as they chatted and smiled and talked to one another in the cheery tones of youth. Their new year was starting out great so far. I smiled as I drove away remembering some of my own past holiday experiences.

Ten days later, when I picked Humphry up from school, his face was flushed and he was coughing. Dr. Milton's office wasn't far out of the way back to the ranch, so I took Humphry to him. Dr. Milton was a slender elderly man. He took Humphry into his examining room. I watched as he took the boy's vitals.

Afterward, Dr. Milton told me, "I'm going to give you some pills for him to take twice a day and a bottle of cough syrup to give a teaspoon of before he goes to bed. Right now, he has a bad cold. But we don't want it to turn into pneumonia. Try to keep him out of the weather as much as possible. I suggest, if possible, give him warm broth or some type of bland soup such as cream of chicken or tomato. And I want to see him again in one week."

I thanked the doctor, paid the bill, and took Humphry on home. I told Mrs. Rayes what the doctor had said, letting her also take charge of the medicines since Humphry stayed in the main house. At her suggestion, I called the school and told Humphry's teacher I was keeping him home for a couple of days.

Humphry didn't like the idea of staying indoors those two days. He thought it was his job to tend to the chickens and to take care of his little mare.

"I'll take care of that, Humphry. You just stay indoors and try to get over that cold," I told him.

I knew that hurt his feelings, but I figured it better to hurt his feelings than for pneumonia to set in.

"You don't need to be getting out in the weather and cause your cold to get worse or for it to turn in to pneumonia."

Humphry gave me a downhearted hurt look, but he said, "Okay."

"Maybe this would be a good time to practice on your guitar," I suggested.

He nodded, and I gave him a hug. He gave me a halfhearted hug, and I knew it was because of his disappointment of having to be inside for the next two days. Two days could seem like a lifetime to a six-year-old.

I had a thought and I told him, "You're pretty good at drawing. Maybe you could draw and paint something for Grandma and Grandpa Rayes."

That brought a slight smile and an agreeable nod. I could see an idea forming by the expression on his young face. Maybe life wasn't so bad after all.

23

During the school's spring break, I took Humphry with me to visit the judge at the courthouse in Buffalo. I wasn't at all sure he would be in, but fortunately he was, and he agreed to see us.

"What do I need to do to see about adopting Humphry?" I asked him.

"The first thing you will need to do, Mr. Cotton, is to fill a Petition for Adoption," he told me.

"Where do I get one of those?" I asked him.

"Let me see if the court attorney is in," he said.

He dialed a number and must have gotten the attorney's office because I heard him tell the person on the other end of the phone to come to his chambers and to bring along a Petition for Adoption and any other necessary adoption documents he might have on hand.

While we waited on the arrival of the attorney, the judge asked Humphry, "Young man, do you agree to this adoption?"

Humphry beamed. I'm sure the smile he gave the judge was the top contender of all of his smiles to date.

"Yes, Your Honor! I love James, and James loves me. And James is my friend!"

"I understand you work on a big ranch near Miami, is that right?" the judge asked.

"Yes, sir. James works for Grandma and Grandpa Rayes. And I have my own room in their house. And I have my own horse. Her name is Lady. James and Uncle Steve broke her for me to ride. And Uncle Lyle is teaching me to play my guitar. And Uncle Bob and Uncle Andy are teaching me how to rope and mend harnesses. And in the mornings, I gather the eggs and feed the chickens for Grandma Rayes before I go to school."

The judge was smiling at Humphry and his excitement, so was the attorney who had come in, just as Humphry started talking to the judge.

Judge Launders introduced the attorney, Milton Hayes, to us. Then he told Attorney Hayes I needed to fill in an application for Petition for Adoption to get the proceedings started for me to adopt Humphry.

The attorney opened his briefcase and extracted a document and handed it to me, along with a pen with which to write. While I was doing that, the judge explained our situation to the attorney, explaining further that we have no information about Humphry's father, who had died some four years ago, and that he would have to see if he could come up with records about Mrs. Hargrove who had been burned to death in the house fire. They would also see if he could come up with a birth certificate for Humphry. Attorney Hayes remarked that he would do everything in his power to come up with the necessary documents. I didn't envy the attorney's job.

When I had filled in the Petition for Adoption, I handed it to the attorney.

"It usually takes between sixty to ninety days to get everything in order for the court hearing for the adoption," he told me. "However, this may take a little longer, depending on what records I can come up with. Does the boy have any relatives besides his older brother?"

I looked at Humphry who shook his head no and replied, "None that we know of, sir. And his brother is wanted for murder of their mother."

Attorney Hayes frowned, looked at Judge Launders, and asked, "Wasn't that young man apprehended a few weeks back down near Fort Supply?"

"I seem to remember something of that sort," the judge commented.

I hadn't heard about Wayne being caught. It was news to me—news I thought justified.

"Is he in jail somewhere?"

"I believe the word is that he is in prison at McAlester for life," Attorney Hayes said.

"Will he have any say in whether or not I can adopt Humphry?" I asked.

"None whatsoever," the attorney told me. "A prisoner with a life sentence has no rights."

"Mr. Cotton, when all the necessary paperwork is done, there will be a social worker who will schedule appointments with you. There will be at least three visits. This is a requirement. They have to inspect the environment in which the child will be living, and you will also need three letters of recommendation from people who can support you and your respectability. I will be in touch with you and let you know when the adoption date will be for you and Humphry to appear here for the verdict. I must also let you know that adoptions are not always accepted. But we'll do everything we can for you and young Humphry," Judge Launders told me.

"Thank you, Your Honor. And thank you, Mr. Hayes. I appreciate everything you are doing for us," I responded.

I put an arm around Humphry as we walked toward the door to go out to my pickup.

Once in the vehicle, Humphry asked me, "James, do you think the judge and that attorney will let you adopt me?"

I could hear the worry in his voice. I didn't need him to be that worried or fearful of being taken from me.

"Hum, I think they will let me adopt you," I told him. "If not, I still have custody of you. But I think they will let me adopt you. It just may take longer than we'd like it to for the attorney to find all the papers he needs and get everything in order. But we live on a large ranch, and I have worked there for nearly ten years. Mr. and Mrs. Rayes are well thought of and honest. And so are my parents out in Guymon. If it becomes necessary, I can tell your teacher about why I registered you in school as Humphry Cotton, and I think she will write a letter of recommendation for me if I need her to. So try not to worry about it. Meantime, let's see about getting something to eat and getting us back to the ranch."

"But why does that social worker need to come see us?" Humphry asked me.

"She has to make a report, Hum, on how she finds the living conditions at the ranch. What type of people she thinks all of us are. And fill in any recommendations she feels necessary for us to apply to our way of life on the report she turns in to the office she works for," I told him.

"Why would we need to change anything about how we live out on the ranch?" he wanted to know.

"I don't know, Humphry. We may not have to change anything. We may qualify for the adoption just the way things are. If we do, she will put that in her first report. Reports after that are what are called 'follow-up reports' that she will fill in as to whether things are still the same or if something has changed in our lives," I answered. "But if she does find something that she feels would better the situation, we will have to do as she suggests."

Humphry gave me an "oh" and fell silent.

Minutes later, we were dining on a fine roast beef dinner in the Carter's Café. Whoever was cooking was almost as good as Mom's and Mrs. Rayes's. And we both ate like we hadn't had food for a week. They followed the meal with a slice of banana cream pie.

I paid for our dinner and then herded us both toward the pickup and headed toward Miami.

* * * * *

It was late when we got back to the ranch. The boss and his wife met us at the door, and the hired hands came inside behind us.

"How'd things go with the judge?" Grant Rayes asked.

I told him what all had transpired and to expect the social worker, who was to call before she came. I also told them I would need letters of recommendation from them, my folks, and a few others who knew me. But I also told them it may take some time for Attorney Hayes to find the records he needs in order to get the adoption papers ready. And as I had already told Humphry, there was no guarantee they would approve the adoption but that I believed they would.

Mr. Rayes assured me he would write one of the letters of recommendation. The crew also agreed that each of them would write one too. I thanked them and let them know I appreciate their support.

"We'll have to be on our toes when that lady from the Social Services comes out," Mrs. Rayes commented. "So I need to get busy and spruce up this house, and, Grant, you and the boys see about getting the barns, shed, and corrals in shape. And don't forget the front yard."

They all laughed, and Grant assured her they would get started on things in the morning.

I didn't see anything wrong with the house. It was always sparkling clean. But I guess women have a knack for knowing what needs to be done. And Lord knows we men had plenty of sprucing up to do outside. By the time the social worker would come, even the corrals would be sparkling clean.

I put an arm around Humphry and said, "Let's go check on Lady."

He turned with me, and we left the house to go to the barn where Lady had spent the day in her stall.

As Humphry gave her grain and began brushing her, I commented, "Humphry, none of us adults have thought about how you feel about the adoption or how you feel about your brother. Now that he has been caught and sent to prison, how do you feel about that, Hum?"

"I'm glad he's in prison, James. He can't hurt me in there, and I won't be getting blamed no more for things that Wayne did," he answered.

"You must still have a few feelings for him. After all, he is your brother," I said.

"James, you're my friend, and I guess if you get to adopt me, that will make you my dad too. But that's okay. I want to be with you, James. And I don't care what they do with Wayne, so long as he can't bother me anymore," he told me with a measure of sentiment in his voice.

"That's all I needed to know, Humphry. Wayne doesn't know where you are. He doesn't know my last name, And he wouldn't be looking for you as Humphry Cotton. I love you, and so does everyone else around here. So you don't need to worry about anything."

24

I sat down a couple nights later and wrote Mom and Dad. I told them about taking Humphry to Buffalo during the school's spring break and what transpired with Judge Launders and the Attorney Milton Hayes. I told them about the letters of recommendation I would need later and asked them if they would mind writing one for me. I also mentioned Mr. and Mrs. Rayes were going to write one for me, and that the rest of the hired hands had also agreed to write letters of recommendation for me. I told them it might take a while before the attorney found the information he needed to proceed with the adoption because there are no records of who Humphry's father was, and the man was buried in an unmarked grave at the Hargrove homestead.

The attorney would have to see if he could find a marriage license of some sort. I didn't know her first name, and neither did young Humphry who had just always called her *mom*. The attorney would also have to have a birth certificate found or have a new one made for Humphry before the adoption hearing could be executed. I let them know that Humphry was glad his brother was now in prison and unable to hurt him. And lastly, I explained that the judge and the attorney had both cautioned that the adoption may not be allowed. It was a fifty-fifty chance.

But I believed they would allow me to adopt Humphry when it was all said and done.

I mailed the letter the next day, then busied myself with helping clean the ranch buildings where needed and doing other things that needed attention. All of us worked tirelessly to make the ranch as presentable as possible so that whenever the social worker came out, she would not have a reason to find fault with anything. Had Mr. Rayes had in mind to sell the ranch, any buyer would have been impressed.

At the end of the week, Grant Rayes sought me out. I was riding fence along the south end of his ranch, and I was a little surprised when he rode up and dismounted. He walked over to me and with concern written all over his face.

"James, once this adoption is over, what do you plan to do?" Mr. Rayes asked.

The question took me by surprise, but I told him, "Unless you fire me, I am going to stay here on the ranch and raise Humphry."

"You're too good of a hand to fire. Besides, if I fire you, the rest of the crew would leave too, and I'd have to hire new men to train in. And I'm gettin' too old to do that," he said.

"Mr. Rayes, you have treated me well over the years. I have no reason to want to quit. Besides, I don't think the rest would leave just because I did—that is, if I were to leave, which I don't plan on doing," I told him.

"Well, I know your folks would have you move back there with them, and you'd have no trouble getting a job. But the rest of the crew have already told me if you leave, they will too," he replied.

"Aw, they're just saying that, Mr. Rayes. They love working for you as much as I do," I said.

"No," he countered. "They mean it. You see, James, they have all become attached to little Humphry too. He has become a part of their family to each of them, and if you were to leave and take him somewhere else, memories of him at this ranch would be too much for them to handle. It would be much easier for them to find a job somewhere else where they don't have to be reminded of the boy every which way they look. Here, the memories would be too painful for them. The wife and I have also became attached to Humphry and he's grown on us just like he has on the rest of the crew. It would be especially hard on Ester because we lost a boy to a rattler when he was about Humphry's age. And Humphry has helped fill that void for her."

"I assure you, we won't be leaving the ranch. They may not allow me to adopt him, but I still have the custody paper the judge signed, and I believe they would have to honor that. I think they will approve the adoption, but if not, we'll cross that bridge when we come to it. In the meantime, Humphry loves it here. This is the only real home he's known. And I see no reason why he can't grow up here," I said.

"Well, I'll ride back to the house with you," he told me.

He was silent on the ride home.

I thought about the other hired hands. They had all been good to Humphry. They had all been guilty of spoiling him at times. To them, he had become the nephew they never had, and they had all accepted him calling them Uncle before he barely know them. But then, Mr. Rayes and his wife had gone along with Humphry calling them Grandma and Grandpa Rayes. I had never known until today that they had lost a son, and neither had I known Mrs. Rayes's first name. I had worked there ten years now and had never known her first name. But then I had never had a reason to know it.

I had not been aware that they had lost a son, but after Mr. Rayes told me what he did, I knew there was no way I could ever leave and take Humphry from them or him from the only real home he had ever known. They were family now and would always be family in their own minds.

We were almost to the house when Mr. Rayes said, "You know, James, I believe God sent you to that boy to deliver him out of that evil situation he lived in. It must have been pretty hard on him to always be accused of things he didn't do, take on chores he wasn't big enough to do, and be abused by the older brother too. And then to know his brother had burned their mother in the house and wouldn't let him try to save her—I believe God meant for you to be with Humphry."

I told Mr. Rayes what Humphry had said about his brother being in prison and about what I had told Humphry.

Mr. Rayes nodded and remarked, "I can't say as I blame him for feeling that way."

At the barn, I took the reins from Mr. Rayes and told him I would put up the horses. He nodded and walked on up to the house. As soon as I got the horses unsaddled and fed, I went on to the house too and was met by a hug and one of those beautiful heart-grabbing smiles from Humphry. It made my day.

"Would you like to hear the new song me and Uncle Lyle can play?" Humphry asked me.

Tired as I was, I couldn't refuse, so I told him, "Sure thing, Humphry. Go get Uncle Lyle. I expect Grandma and Grandpa Rayes would like to hear it too."

I didn't have to tell him twice. He was off like a flash and, moments later, came back with Uncle Lyle and his guitar. We listened as they played the new song and others as well.

After Lyle went back to the bunkhouse, Mrs. Rayes told her husband that Bob and Lyle had cleaned up the garden area and planted the seeds for this summer's vegetables.

"You'll have to check it out in the morning, Grant. They did a real good job of it. And Humphry helped them with the planting," she told him proudly, beaming at Humphry. I had a notion that from now on, when it was said that "Humphry did it!" it would be with a positive attitude and about the things for which everyone could be proud of him for doing.

The garden was the last place that needed attention. Now that it was done, the ranch was—if I might beam myself—in immaculate condition. I couldn't remember it being so cleaned and spruced up in all the ten years I had worked here. I thought to myself that it could have won one of those home beautification contests, hands down, or maybe won Ranch of the Year.

That weekend, Tracy Matthews came by to talk to the boss about some cattle. He also wanted to see about buying a couple of the horses Steve and I had trained. Both were geldings, one a sorrel and the other a buckskin. Steve and I had trained them for cattle, and both were good horses.

Matthews was impressed by the look of the ranch, commenting, "If I'm going to keep up with the Joneses, so to speak, I guess I better get my crew busy on clean up detail at my place."

"It gave the boys something to do during the slack time," Mr. Rayes told him.

"That's a good idea, Grant. I guess we get busy with other things and don't really think about cleaning up around the homeplace. I'll have to get my Three Bar M crew busy and get my place back in shape," he said.

25

Three weeks later, Mrs. Rayes received a call from a social worker at the courthouse in Miami. I wasn't at the house when the call came in, so Mrs. Rayes took the message for me. The woman had set an appointment for me to meet with her at the ranch the following Tuesday around ten in the morning. Humphry still had ten days of school before they let out for the summer, so I suspected the social worker wanted to check me out and also get some idea of what kind of living conditions Humphry was in. Mrs. Rayes thought the same thing. She and her husband would be on hand when the lady arrived.

She drove up in a fairly new tan Chevy and brought a clipboard to the house with her. I thought I also saw a small camera with her. No doubt she wanted to take photos of the outside of the ranch yard, probably the inside of the house too, and maybe also the room where Humphry stayed at the house. She rang the doorbell, and Mrs. Rayes answered and told her to come on in.

"I'm Ellen Shores," she said by way of introduction.

Mrs. Rayes introduced her to the rest of us.

She shook hands, and Mrs. Rayes asker her, "Won't you sit down, Miss Shores? Would you like some coffee?"

"Coffee please," Miss Shores said as she laid her clipboard in front of her on the table and began to remove a page from it.

"Mr. Cotton, I wanted to visit with you without the boy being present and get to know you a little better. I have been enlightened about your circumstance and told you want to adopt the child. Is that correct?" she asked me.

Mrs. Rayes set her coffee down near her and seated herself next to Mr. Rayes a couple seats down at the table.

"Yes, ma'am, it is," I answered.

"Have you worked here long?" she wanted to know.

"Yes, ma'am. Just a little over ten years."

She lifted her eyebrows at that. I guess she hadn't expected me to have been employed anywhere for that long.

"What is your primary job here?" she asked.

"I train horses for Mr. Rayes, but I also help with the cattle and whatever else he needs me to do for him," I answered.

"How old are you, Mr. Cotton?"

That question surprised me, but I answered her, "Twenty-eight, ma'am."

"Are you married? Or have you ever been married?" she asked.

To which I answered, "No."

"How did you come to meet this boy?" she inquired.

I told her about riding onto the Hargrove place to ask if I could water my horse and fill my canteen.

"You were riding a horse? Wouldn't it have been faster to drive to wherever you were going?" she questioned.

Her face had taken on a mask of disbelief as though she thought I was lying to her.

I went on to explain that I did not have a vehicle at the time and I had bought a stallion from Mr. Rayes that I wanted to take to my Dad out in Guymon, so I rode the horse across country. I again told her I had stopped at the Hargrove place to see if I could water my horse and fill my canteen. I went on to tell her young Humphry was at the corral watching young foals play. I had joined them until his mother came out and got after him for talking to a stranger. I also explained the woman was a widow and all but out of groceries, needed some fences repaired, and needed to be able to let the mares out of their stalls in the barn so they could graze.

"So you felt like it was your place to interfere and help her out even though she told you to leave?" she said, sounding more like a disapproving statement than a question.

"Miss Shores, any other man who was half a man even would have done the same thing for her and her boys," I told her.

"Boys? Did she have more than one?" she asked.

I told her about Wayne—his shiftless ways; his blaming things on his younger brother; and how, sometime after I left, he had hit his mother and knocked her down, burned the house, and refused to let the younger brother try to get their mother out of the house.

"How horrible! Where is the older boy now?" she wanted to know.

I explained to her he had been given a life sentence and sent to Oklahoma State Penitentiary in McAlester.

"I came back by their place on my way back from Guymon and finally found Humphry. He had hidden in the hay loft in the barn. I took him to town, got him cleaned up and into some clean clothes, fed him, and brought him home to the ranch. Mr. and Mrs. Rayes graciously let me keep him here and even let him have his own room here in the main house," I explained to the social worker. "Before that, I also stopped by the courthouse in Buffalo and talked to Judge Launders about what I had found at the Hargrove place. I figured he might want to put Humphry with the Department of Human Services. Instead, he and the sheriff talked, and he asked Humphry if he wanted to stay with me. When the boy said he did, the judge called in an attorney and signed custody of Humphry over to me and had an all-points bulletin issued for his brother."

"I see," she said. "And you have the boy in school in Miami?"

"Yes, ma'am, although I enrolled him as Humphry Cotton instead of his own last name as a safety measure in case his brother, who was still at large, was trying to find him to do him some harm," I told her.

"Has he been to a doctor for a physical?" she wanted to know.

"No, ma'am. Only for a cold he came down with this last winter," I said.

Miss Shores looked thoughtful for a few minutes during which time Mrs. Rayes refilled all our coffee cups.

As she picked up the paper she had taken from the clipboard and returned it, she said, "I'd like to see his room, if I may."

I walked her down the hall to Humphry's room. She took photos of it and commented on how nice it was.

We came back into the kitchen, and the social worker told me I would need to get Humphry a physical prior to the hearing date for the adoption. Other than that, she thought probably there would be no complications with the adoption—more so, she said, because this was a special case. She told me she would have to make at least two more visits to the ranch before the hearing date.

"I forgot to ask you your birth date and where you were born," she said.

I told her, and she made quick notes on the edge of the paper she had returned to the clipboard.

"Another thing—do you and the child attend church?" she asked.

"Yes, ma'am. We go every Sunday. We attend the First Methodist Church in Miami," I told her.

That seemed to satisfy her. She decided to leave then. I walked her out to her vehicle. She took photos of the ranch yard and buildings.

She turned to me and said, "I'm glad I met you, Mr. Cotton. You seem like a really nice person. The next time I come out, I imagine will be after school lets out, and I can visit Humphry then also. I might add that the people you work for seem really nice also."

I thanked her, and she got into her car and left. I stood watching her drive away thinking she had been a little stuffy. But maybe that was what her job called for.

26

The next day, I went by Dr. Milton's office and had him schedule an appointment for a complete physical for Humphry. Dr. Milton scheduled it for July 25th at 9:30 a.m. That would be after school let out and before the next visit from Miss Shores was due at the ranch. And by then, Dr. Milton said he would have the report ready so I could give a copy of it to her.

When I told Humphry about it, he wanted to know, "Why do I have to have a physical done, James?"

"Because the social worker has to know you are in good physical condition and that there is nothing in your system that could affect you later on in your life—things we don't know about right now such as blood disease or circulation problems. And it's better we find out now than later on. I'm sure you will get a clean bill of health, but it doesn't hurt to be sure," I told him.

I wasn't good at explaining things like that, and I wasn't completely sure that Humphry understood it at his age.

But he only commented, "Oh, okay."

I made it a point to call Judge Launders in Buffalo and fill him in on what had happened so far and asked him if he or the attorney had been able to find out anything on Humphry's parents or were able to have a birth certificate made for him.

When I stopped long enough for the judge to answer my questions, he told me my case had been transferred to Judge Marcus Holmstead in Miami who, as far as he knew, had found nothing about the boy's father and very little about the birth mother but did learn from some of the merchants in the little town near where the Hargroves lived that her first name was Olivia.

"At least we have that much to go on," he said, further stating they could create a new birth certificate from that for Humphry. "You should have it in two or three weeks."

I thanked him. Hopefully the new birth certificate would get to me by the time, or shortly after, I was able to get a copy of Humphry's medical report.

* * * * *

In the days that followed, I broke a young buckskin stud colt and gray filly.

The buckskin was a good-looking colt. I liked the way he held himself proudly and the way he moved. He had a manner of intelligence to him. He took easily to the halter and to the saddle, and I was hopeful that Mr. Rayes would geld him and keep him for the ranch.

The gray filly took a little longer to break. She was cautious of everything and not sure she wanted any part of any of it. But working with her slowly and talking to her as I did calmed her down some. It took an extra two days with her before she came to trust me. But once she did, she calmed down all the way. She took the bridle easily and the saddle, though she wasn't sure about me mounting her the first time.

I worked with her on that a few minutes before I actually mounted her. She stood, not moving, until I touched her sides with my boots. She gave a few half-hearted bucks and quit. She would be among the horses sold later on when Steve and I had enough broke that Mr. Rayes could load in the big trailer and take to the sale barn.

Steve and I were also in on bringing in a herd of heifers to sort for the sale, along with Bob and Andy. Lyle helped us sort and brand the baby calves before we sorted the cow–calf pairs back and took them to another pasture. But mostly, he and young Humphry were busy with keeping the barn and corrals cleaned out and keeping the yard cleaned and the garden weeded.

* * * * *

HUMPHRY DID IT!

I took young Humphry to his doctor's appointment. It didn't take as long as I had expected.

Humphry hadn't known what to expect, but he followed Dr. Milton and did everything the doctor told him to do. Dr. Milton explained everything he did, even the shots he gave him last. He and the good doctor became friends, and I was glad. That would make it much easier on all of us on future visits.

Humphry seemed to be on a growing spurt. It wasn't long after school let out that I had to take him to town and get new clothes and boots for him. The only thing I didn't have to replace yet was his cowboy hat. He looked sharp in his new outfits.

Dr. Milton had come into the store, and when he saw us, he came to where we were looking at some new shirts for Humphry.

He handed me an envelope telling me, "I saw you come into the store so I thought I'd give you these medical reports for Humphry so you'll have them when the social worker comes to visit you again. I know you will be happy to know the boy has a clean bill of health."

Humphry grinned, and I told Dr. Milton, "Thank you, sir. Why don't you come out to the ranch and have supper with us? I'm sure Mrs. Rayes wouldn't mind. And you can listen to Humphry and Lyle play for us. Humphry is pretty good with his guitar now."

Dr. Milton seemed pleased, and he commented, "I might just do that. I didn't know the boy could play."

"Uncle Lyle has been teaching me," Humphry spoke up with a smile.

I knew he welcomed the chance to play for someone who hadn't heard him yet.

We left the store a few minutes later with Humphry's new wardrobe and went back to the ranch. I told Mrs. Rayes about inviting Dr. Milton for supper, and she smiled and told me that was okay.

Turning to Humphry, she said, "My, don't you look nice! Can I see the rest of your new outfits?"

"Sure, Grandma! Come on!" Humphry exclaimed, heading toward his room.

I found Mr. Rayes checking his stock trailer. It was already spotless from the wash job he had given it. And as far as I could see, all the tires were good. As I walked up, he told me to go stand behind the trailer.

"Let me know if the lights are working properly," he said.

They were, and I told him so. I also told him Humphry now was the proud owner of a new wardrobe of clothing and that Dr. Milton had given him a clean bill of health. I explained that Dr. Milton had sent a copy of Humphry's medical records home with me.

I added, "Dr. Milton will be coming to supper tonight. He wants to listen to Humphry play his guitar."

Mr. Rayes nodded and said, "Well then, son, I guess we better tell the rest of the boys so they will have time to get cleaned up. Besides, today is Humphry's birthday. He'll be a big boy of seven now."

I had forgotten. Yes, today is Humphry's seventh birthday. I guess his new clothes were a good birthday gift, and so was his clean bill of health. I felt embarrassed about forgetting.

Mr. Rayes rounded up the rest of the hired hands.

"Boys, since this is Humphry's birthday and he will be seven, you boys need to take time to get yourselves cleaned up. Besides, Dr. Milton will be dining with us. So, Lyle, we will expect you and Humphry to do a program after supper."

I watched as sheepish grins took their place on each man's face. I think they too had forgotten Humphry's birthday. They nodded to the boss and began to gather their clean clothes, and towels for their showers, and their shaving gear.

Mrs. Rayes had outdone herself to fix supper which included freshly sliced tomatoes from the garden.

Dr. Milton arrived a few minutes early and was offered a seat in the living room with Mr. Rayes. They visited until the hired hands began trickling into the house. Lyle brought his guitar and stood it next to the fireplace.

"After supper, we'll have a little music, Dr. Milton. Lyle here has been teaching Humphry to play, and the kid is pretty good," Mr. Rayes told the doctor.

"I'll look forward to listening," Dr. Milton commented.

We had just started eating when we heard a knock on the door. Mrs. Rayes answered it and came back to the table with Miss Shores following her.

HUMPHRY DID IT!

"You guys scoot down and find another chair for our guest," Mrs. Rayes said.

"I didn't mean to interrupt your meal," Miss Shores apologized.

"We were just getting started. So fill your plate and join us. This is Humphry's birthday, so leave room for cake and ice cream," Mrs. Rayes told her.

The rest of us resumed eating. And while we ate, I introduced Miss Shores to Humphry, the doctor, and the hired hands. She blushed but told them all she was glad to meet them.

"When we get through eating, I will get you the copy of Humphry's medical transcript. Dr. Milton said he has a clean bill of health," I told the social worker.

"I'm not here on official business. I just thought I'd come out and meet the boy and maybe get to know him a little better. But I'm glad I came. This has been a terrific meal," she stated.

"Wait until you hear Lyle and Humphry play," Mrs. Rayes offered. "They are quite a pair of musicians."

Humphry beamed as he did anytime one or the other of Mr. and Mrs. Rayes complimented him, and he brought forth one of those heartwarming smiles and looked straight at Miss Shores. He had been quiet the whole meal, and I think she was surprised by his smile.

"Me and Uncle Lyle are going to play and sing a few songs as soon as we all get through eating. I'm glad you and Dr. Milton could come this evening," he told her.

"I'm sure I will enjoy it," she commented.

Moments later, she was sitting in the living room, with the rest of us listening to Humphry and Lyle.

Hum had learned a couple more songs now, and they played them. I think just to test his skill, Lyle began playing one he hadn't yet taught Humphry. But Humphry picked up on it quickly and finished playing it with Uncle Lyle.

Afterward, I walked Miss Shores to her car and got the medical papers on Humphry out of my pickup and gave them to her.

"Humphry plays quite well and sings well too, for one his age," she said.

I thanked her and told her his birth certificate should be here in a few days.

Dr. Milton stayed a while longer visiting with the men, something he didn't get a chance to do often and something they didn't get to do often either.

I helped Mrs. Rayes clean up the kitchen, and while we were doing that, Mrs. Rayes made the comment, "James, I don't think that young lady came here tonight to meet Humphry and get to know him a little better. I rather thought she acted like she came here to be nosy to see if she could catch us all unaware of something she could use to prevent the adoption. I hope that's not the case, but you be careful, James. We don't need to give her any thread of evidence she could use against you."

"I had the same feeling, Mrs. Rayes. And I noticed she didn't talk to Humphry until he told her him and Lyle were going to play and sing songs. To me that didn't seem like wanting 'to get to know him,' as she put it," I agreed.

The following week, the new birth certificate for Humphry came in the mail. I had expected them to call me to come pick it up, but they didn't. I made a trip into town to get a copy of it made so that I would also have a copy of it after I gave the mailed copy to Miss Shores.

She was to have scheduled another visit to the ranch. So far, she had not done so. That made me all the more suspicious about her visit to the ranch on the evening of Humphry's birthday.

I stopped at the courthouse to have the copy of his birth certificate made. The lady in the records office made it for me. I thanked her and asked her where I could find Marcus Holmstead. She told me his office was on the second floor but cautioned he might be in court.

I thanked her again and headed toward the stairs.

When I reached second floor, I was met by two security guards who immediately wanted to know what business I had on that floor.

"I would like to talk to the judge, if possible," I answered them.

"What about?" one of the security guards asked.

"I have applied for an adoption of a young boy, and I just wanted to check with him to find out if there has been a hearing date set as yet," I told him.

"The judge is in court this afternoon, sir. Your best bet would be to come back tomorrow morning. But if you want to leave your name and a phone number, I will see if I can have him call you later on this afternoon," the security guard said, handing me a piece of paper and a pencil.

I wrote down my name and the phone number for the ranch house and thanked him.

"You bet," he commented.

As I walked back toward my pickup, I developed a nagging feeling that I needed to get an extra copy of Humphry's medical report from Dr. Milton. I didn't know why that thought had come to me, but I followed my instinct and went to Dr. Milton's office. He greeted me warmly, although a little puzzled by my visit.

I explained to him about getting Humphry's birth certificate copied so I'd have a copy at the ranch in case I ever needed it. I also told him I need to come back tomorrow morning to visit Judge Marcus Holmstead, and I asked him if I could possibly get another copy of Humphry's medical report as I had given the one he gave me to the social worker for her records.

Dr. Milton agreed to have a copy of Humphry's medical records ready for me to pick up in the morning. Then he said something I was totally not expecting.

"That young woman is up to no good, James. Unless I miss my bet, I'd guess she is going to try to take Humphry away from you. Her visit the other night wasn't a social call, I dare say. So you be careful what you say and do around her. Don't give her anything she can use against you."

"Thanks, Doc. I'll be careful. Everyone at the ranch got the same impression, including me. We think that woman is up to something no good too," I told him.

I came out of the doctor's office and almost ran slap into Lyle.

"What are you doing in town, Lyle?" I asked him.

"Trying to catch up with you," he stated.

"I was just about to go back to the ranch. Is there something wrong?" I asked.

"Yes, James. Humphry's gone, and I knew you didn't bring him to town with you. So Mr. Rayes told me to come in and find you and get you back out to the ranch," he told me.

"Maybe I should stop by the sheriff's office on the way," I said.

"Wouldn't hurt," was his answer. "I'll follow you and we can drive back together."

HUMPHRY DID IT!

At the sheriff's office, the man with the star introduced himself as Stanley Foley.

I explained to him about Humphry and also about the coming adoption and my appointment in the morning with the judge. Lyle took it from there to tell him about the folks at the ranch discovering Humphry missing about half an hour before.

"I can't do anything to help you until the boy has been missing for twenty-four hours," Sheriff Foley said. "If he isn't found by the time you come back to see the judge in the morning, Mr. Cotton, come back by here, and we'll go from there."

"Thank you, Sheriff. I just wanted to let you know he's missing in case you see him somewhere. Hopefully I won't have to come see you tomorrow," I replied.

Lyle and I returned to the ranch to find horses saddled and ready to go. We knew before we got out of our vehicles the rest of the day would be on horseback combing the ranch for the missing child.

We searched every possible nook and cranny—every watering hole, every rock cliff, every spectacular, beautiful place, every trail, and every tree that was big enough to climb. We came in at sundown neither finding hide nor hair nor any trace of Humphry.

When I had unsaddled and put up my horse and tackle, I went into the house and checked Humphry's room. It was tidy as always, but his guitar was missing.

I went back into the living room where Mr. and Mrs. Rayes were and asked permission to use their phone. Mrs. Rayes wanted to know whom I was calling.

"The sheriff," I told her. "I need him to check with that social worker's office and see if he can get the address for Ellen Shores."

"Ellen Shores? Why, James, what do you need her address for?" she asked.

I told them then about having to see the judge in the morning, that I had Humphry's birth certificate copied so that I myself will have a copy of it, and about asking Dr. Milton to make me another copy of his medical records.

"And," I added, "Ellen Shores was the only person besides us to go into Humphry's room. On top of that, she listened with the rest of us to him and Lyle play and sing after his birthday supper, after which we all had the feeling that she was not there just to socialize but may have had an ulterior motive for dropping in unannounced like she did. She hardly spoke to Humphry and didn't even wish him a happy birthday."

Mr. and Mrs. Rayes looked at each other, and Mr. Rayes commented, "I hadn't thought of that, but she didn't wish the kid happy birthday. And you're right, James, we all had the feeling after she left that she was up to no good. On top of that, Humphry did sometimes leave his guitar down at the bunkhouse with Lyle's so he could practice without disturbing the rest of us. It wouldn't have been hard to kidnap him from there without being seen. Go ahead and call the sheriff."

I called Sheriff Foley, and after telling him we had searched every square inch of the ranch, we had finally concluded that Humphry had been kidnapped. I asked him if he could find out the address of that social worker so I could go by and talk to her and see if she had Humphry. He told me he would see what he could come up with. I thanked him.

"I should have taken him with me when I went to town this morning. If I had, this wouldn't have happened," I said sullenly.

"Now, James. You can't blame it on yourself. When you left this morning, Humphry was weeding the garden. And besides, I could have been looking after him better myself," Mrs. Rayes said.

"But he's my responsibility. And he may be out there somewhere, hurt. And besides how responsible will this look at the adoption hearing?" I replied.

Mr. Rayes got up and came over to me. He put a hand on my shoulder and said, "Stop beating yourself up, James. Humphry will be found. We have good law enforcement in Miami. They'll turn him up somewhere."

I nodded. I felt terrible. I had let Humphry down. I loved that little cuss, and I had never in my wildest dreams thought we'd come across a day like this. I should have taken him to town with me. But I hadn't. And now I had to live with the guilt of not doing so and with the fear that whoever had taken him may have hurt him physically and mentally.

"Come on. Let's get out of Mom's way so she can get supper ready," he said, turning me toward the door.

We wandered down toward the barn, and I brushed Humphry's little mare and gave her some grain. It gave me something to do while fighting back my tears.

28

It was with a heavy heart that I showered and shaved and got myself ready to go to the courthouse that morning. I had slept fitfully during the night, thinking of what might have happened to Humphry and berating myself for letting it happen. My attitude that morning was in the depth of despair on the bottom level.

I reached for the door of my pickup, but Mr. Rayes was there, telling me, "I'll drive, James."

I handed him the key and went around to the other side and let myself into the cab of the pickup. We didn't talk on the way into Miami. Once in town, though, I asked him to stop at Dr. Milton's office first so I could pick up my copy of Humphry's medical records.

"Have you heard anything yet on the whereabouts of the boy?" Dr. Milton asked me.

I told him no.

At the courthouse, we found a parking place, and as soon as I retrieved the rest of the documents on Humphry from the glove box, we went inside. Inside down the long hallway to the courtroom, Sheriff Foley caught up with us. He said he wanted to go in with us to see Judge Holmstead. While we waited to be let into the courtroom, Sheriff Foley told us he had found Ellen Shores's address yesterday evening.

"I got a search warrant and took a deputy with me to her house. Miss Shores was hateful and nasty with me and my deputy, but a search of her house found Humphry locked in a bedroom toward the back of her house. The deputy busted in the door and found young Humphry. I arrested Miss Shores. I have her at the jailhouse. I took the boy home with me for the night. He is at my office. I'll bring him up in a few minutes. But I wanted to talk to Judge Holmstead first."

"Is Humphry okay?" I asked Sheriff Foley.

"Yes. He's okay. She didn't hurt him. He was just scared and upset about being away from you," the sheriff told me.

"Thank you," I said with a feeling of relief flooding through my body.

Nothing bad had happened to Humphry physically. But I knew he would have some mental issues to overcome with this experience. I hoped I had the patience to deal with them. I heard footsteps in the hallway and looked up to see the rest of the Slant T hands walking toward us, complete with the boss's wife.

"Well, Rayes, it looks like you brought your whole outfit in," the sheriff commented.

"They came of their own accord. I had nothing to do with it. But they're here to support James. That's the way my men are. They all support each other," Grant Rayes replied.

The security guard at the entrance of the courtroom asked us to step back so the people inside the courtroom could get out. We moved out of the way. Once the last person was out of the courtroom, the security guard told us we could enter. All of us went to the front row of seats, except Sheriff Foley. He went on around to the judge's chambers and entered. It seemed like forever before he came out again. Actually, it was only ten minutes. He came around to where I was sitting and told me he would be back in a few minutes; he was going to go down to his office and bring Humphry to the courtroom.

The judge entered the courtroom just in time to witness Humphry yell, "James!" and run into my arms, wrapping his own around me.

I hugged him to me. I can't tell you what a relief it was to have him with me again. Humphry had tears of joy sliding down his cheeks, and I felt a couple slide down my face too.

"James Cotton, would you please step forward?" the judge summoned.

I stood before him at his bench.

"I was told you want to adopt this boy. Do you have his medical documents with you and a copy of his birth certificate?"

"Yes, Your Honor," I answered, handing the papers to him.

Judge Holmstead read over the records, then turned his attention to Grant Rayes.

"Grant, you are a man well thought of in our community. I understand Mr. Cotton has worked for you a number of years. How would you rate his performance?"

Mr. Rayes came forward and said, "Excellent, Your Honor."

"Did it upset you when he brought the boy home unannounced last year?" the judge inquired.

"No, Your Honor. James had called us from Buffalo and explained the circumstances to us."

That was the first lie I had known my boss to tell!

"He had also intended to hire a babysitter for him," Mr. Rayes continued. "We didn't let him do that. The youngster is a good child. He doesn't give any of us any problems. He's polite and always asks if there's anything he can do to help. He learns quickly and he doesn't complain. My wife and I have grown fond of him, and so have my ranch hands. My Slant T ranch is the first place Humphry has had for a decent home. I think I can speak for all of us in saying we think James should be allowed to adopt Humphry."

Judge Holmstead shuffled the papers in front of him then looked at the hired hands and ask, "Do you gentlemen agree with Mr. Rayes's statement?"

Bob answered for all of them, "Yes we do."

Again the judge shuffled the papers, pulled one, and laid it aside. With the index finger of his right hand, the judge seemed to be reading the paper.

Moments later, he said, "It says here that when Miss Shores conducted her interview at the ranch with Mr. Cotton, he was dirty and unkempt, that the main house left a lot to be desired from the condition she found it in, and that the provisions were scanty and that the outside of the house was rundown. Says she went out later to meet the child and found him in rags and in what she termed undesirable conditions. What can you tell me about that report?"

"I can answer that, Your Honor," Sheriff Stanley Foley told the judge. "That report is an outright lie. I have Miss Shores in my jail downstairs for kidnapping the child a few nights ago in an attempt

HUMPHRY DID IT!

to keep Mr. Cotton from being able to adopt him. She thought she could get by with reporting lies and thus be able later on to adopt him herself."

"May I say something, Your Honor?" Dr. Milton asked.

Judge Holmstead nodded and told the doctor to go ahead.

"Your Honor, I was also with the Rayes family the evening Miss Shores visited. Their house is immaculate. The people were clean and well dressed, including the boy. And Mrs. Rayes is the best cook in the county. And the outside area was clean, including the barns and sheds. If you would question my statement, then perhaps Mr. Rayes will invite you to visit his ranch so you can see for yourself," Dr. Milton stated.

The judge didn't comment. Instead, he asked Humphry if he would like to be adopted by James Cotton and carry the name Humphry Cotton the rest of his life.

Humphry turned on one of those beautiful, heartwarming smiles of his and said, "Yes, Your Honor, I would."

Judge Marcus Holmstead smiled, looked directly at that beaming little face and that wonderful smile, and said, "Okay."

To Sheriff Foley, he said, "Round up the court attorney, and we'll get the adoption done."

Turning back to our boss, the judge commented, "Grant you seem to have some very good ranch hands. Usually there's one or two that don't get along as well as these men do. How do you manage it?"

"Humphry did it!" Mr. Rayes answered. "The boy stole all of our hearts and brought us around to a family-style relationship. He has made a difference in all of our lives. All of us love him, and he loves all of us."

"Which of the men is your foreman?" Judge Holmstead asked.

"I don't need a foreman, Judge. The men get up in the mornings and figure out among themselves what needs to be done, and then they do it," Mr. Rayes told him.

The judge looked up as the court attorney came into the room.

"Let's get these papers signed and notarized and let this adoption be finalized," he told the attorney.

I had to sign a few pages, and Mr. Rayes witnessed them; and then the attorney notarized them for me. The judge looked the papers over and added his signature and told the attorney to run me a copy of them.

He came around the bench and stopped before Humphry.

"Young man," he said, "I am proud to call you Humphry Cotton. It has been a pleasure meeting you, and I hope we will have a lifelong friendship."

Humphry smiled and asked, "Would you like to come out to the ranch and listen to me and Uncle Lyle play our guitars?"

"Why, yes, I would," Judge Holmstead agreed.

"Can you make it this coming Sunday for dinner with us?" Mr. Rayes asked.

"I will be there," the judge told him.

29

When we unloaded back at the ranch, Steve was the first to come to me with an arm outstretched to shake my hand and congratulate me on the adoption.

"I'm glad the adoption went through for you," he said. "Now I don't have to worry about losing my nephew."

The rest of the crew followed his example as Bob, Andy, and then Lyle came to shake my hand and congratulate me.

Mr. and Mrs. Rayes both gave me a hug while the crew took turns hugging their nephew.

"Grandma Rayes, I'll go gather the eggs just as soon as I put my guitar up," Humphry said breaking the hugging and handshaking session.

"Okay, Hum," she told him. "And I guess I'd better go fix breakfast for your uncles and your grandpa and you and your dad."

Bob, who usually was a soft spoken, commented, "Boss, I guess with us all being Humphry's uncles, that makes us all your sons and all of us brothers."

He was smiling as he said it, and his eyes were twinkling as he watched young Humphry go inside the house to put up his guitar.

Andy, not to be outdone, smiled and said, "Now we can call Mr. and Mrs. Rayes Mom and Dad instead of boss."

Lyle, who hadn't said anything so far other than to congratulate me on the adoption, looked at the rest of us and told us, "Just think, boys, now Mr. and Mrs. Rayes have a bunch of knot-headed sons to raise cane with."

"Well, how about if you knot-headed sons get a few chores done while Mom is fixing a bite of breakfast for us?" Mr. Rayes suggested.

Truthfully, it was closer to dinnertime. But whatever Mrs. Rayes put on the table would be fine with all of us.

"I'm going to go in and call my folks," I told them, "and then I'll be out to help you guys."

My parents were both happy about me getting to adopt Humphry, and they asked if I could bring him to visit them before school started again. I told them I'd see if Mr. Rayes could let me have the time off, maybe for a week. The rest of the men needed time off too. I think they had forfeited their time off the year before because of me bringing Humphry to the ranch.

And it wasn't fair to them to do without their time off again this year. I said as much to Dad, and he asked if Mr. Rayes would object to him and Mom visiting the ranch after the hay was cut and baled for a couple of weeks so they could get to know Humphry a little better. I told him I didn't think the boss would object, but I'd ask him. Dad told me I could write them a letter and let them know what Mr. Rayes said about them visiting. I told him okay and ended the conversation.

I asked Mr. Rayes about my parents coming to the ranch to visit. His reply was, "They can come anytime they want to and stay as long as they want to. I like your parents, and Humphry needs to get to know them."

Judge Marcus Holmstead arrived shortly after church let out. We beat him home by maybe twenty minutes. He climbed out of his car, stood a few minutes looking around, and then went to the house. It was as though his mind was countermanding the reports Miss Shores, who was now spending her time in the Miami jail waiting for her day in court, had written about the Slant T ranch. He found it completely opposite of what she had written in her report. The yard and the buildings were still clean and pleasing to gaze upon. What litter there was about the corrals was trifling.

He knocked and was greeted by Mrs. Rayes who ushered him into the living room with her husband. Grant Rayes rose from his chair and shook hands with the Judge and invited him to sit down.

"Your place and your house are nice, Mr. Rayes," the judge told him. "Quite different than that young lady wrote in her report."

"If you'd like, Your Honor, we can take a tour of the buildings and corrals while my wife is preparing lunch," Mr. Rayes told him.

"Okay. I have an idea they are clean too, but I'd like to see them," the judge accepted.

At the bunkhouse, only Andy remained to finish what he had been doing. The bunkhouse itself was clean, and every bed was made. The judge was somewhat surprised as he had always heard bunkhouses were smelly and not necessarily as kept up with as ours had been.

Andy spoke to the judge who returned his greeting.

When they came out to the corrals, I was working with an overo paint gelding, and Steve was working with a white filly, Judge Holmstead seemed to enjoy watching as he and the boss lingered at the corral I was working in and then at the corral Steve was working in. I glanced at him and Mr. Rayes once and thought to myself that they seemed to be enjoying watching me work with the paint. But then I turned my attention back to the horse. I couldn't afford to let the colt think I wasn't paying attention to him. To do so was an invitation to getting myself hurt. This particular gelding was nearly sixteen hands tall, and he was well muscled. I had worked with him enough that he was starting to trust me, and I certainly didn't need any mishaps with him.

Bob and Lyle had ridden out to check the cattle on the home pasture to check for any newborn calves. They would be back in time for dinner.

Humphry had taken a basket and gone to the garden to bring in some vegetables for Mrs. Rayes to fix to go with dinner. He came back with potatoes, radishes, carrots, and tomatoes. Mrs. Rayes had fixed some deviled eggs that morning before church and put a roast in the oven to cook while we were at church. She elected to bake the potatoes and scrub the radishes, slice the tomatoes, and scrub and cut the carrots into carrot sticks. Yesterday, she had fixed a lemon pudding that would become dessert for today's dinner. Fresh homemade bread made yesterday adorned the table, along with a bowl of fresh butter. And she had made both tea and lemonade.

Humphry helped her set the table.

Bob and Lyle were back in time to eat with the rest of us. Steve and I had turned the horses we were working with back into the pasture.

"You're right about one thing," the judge commented. "Your wife is the best cook in this county."

"I'm sure some of the other wives are good cooks too," Mrs. Rayes replied.

Judge Holmstead smiled and told her, "Then I may have to visit every ranch in the county for Sunday dinners to see if I can find them."

Dinner was a success, and there wasn't much by way of leftovers. Talk was of anything that didn't pertain to the courtroom or politics.

Finally, the judge looked at Humphry and asked, "Young man, are you too full to let me listen to some of your music?"

Humphry gave the Judge one of his best smiles, shook his head no, and said, "Let me and Uncle Lyle get our guitars!"

The rest of us moved into the living room. Mr. Rayes carried some of the chairs from the table to the living room to make sure there was room for everyone to sit. He made sure his wife joined the rest of us to listen to the performance by Humphry and Lyle. Usually, she busied herself in the kitchen and listened from there. But not today. Not with Judge Holmstead here.

It only took a few minutes for Lyle and Humphry to get their instruments and begin to play and sing for the rest of us. They entertained us for the next three hours, during which time the judge seemed to thoroughly enjoy himself. He told them afterward that he enjoyed listening to them and asked if he could come back sometime to listen to them again.

Mr. Rayes told him, "Of course you can. You can come any time you want to."

Judge Holmstead thanked him, and after that, he became a regular once a month or so visitor at the Slant T ranch.

30

In the years that followed, Humphry learned the cattle, fencing, and ranch work. His grades were As and Bs at school. He became more accomplished with his guitar, so much so that Judge Marcus Holmstead began to sponsor him in playing engagements—some of which Lyle also accompanied him, others by himself. No one could have been prouder of him than I was.

During the first part of summer, my parents would come get him and take him to Guymon for a couple of weeks. By the time he was fifteen, Dad had found a place for him to play a performance in Guymon every June. Always, Dad would proudly announce the entertainer of the evening as, "My Grandson, Humphry Cotton, ladies and gentlemen!"

He and Mom, as well as Andy and Janet Simmons, fell in love with Humphry. And they all encouraged him in his music. It helped that Humphry liked all of them too, and he liked the fact that Dad let him ride Gunner while visiting with them.

The summer he turned sixteen, I taught him to drive my pickup and took him to get his driver's license, and we also applied for his social security card. Now he could drive himself to his musical engagements and wherever else he needed to go. I also took out a medical insurance for him. I hoped he wouldn't need it, but one never knows and it is always best to be prepared. Plus, he had become interested in training horses with me and Steve. He was leaning some toward rodeo and steer-roping events. I was thankful he had not decided on bull riding.

Andy sought me out one day and asked, "Why don't you talk to Humphry about recording his music?"

"I don't know any recording studios, Andy. But that's an idea. Maybe the judge will know someone in that business. I'll ask Humphry if he'd want to do that, and if he does, we can go from there," I replied.

"He's turned out to be a really good kid, James. I think all of us are as proud of him as you are," he said.

I thanked Andy for his suggestion. I hadn't thought of Humphry recording his music. I was fairly sure Humphry himself hadn't thought of it either.

Later that evening, I found Humphry brushing Lady, and I asked him, "Humphry, have you ever thought of recording some of your music?"

"No, it hadn't entered my mind. I have begun trying to write some lyrics and the music to them. But I haven't thought about recording them," he told me.

"I don't know where a recording studio is around Miami. But if you decide you want to try that, I'll check around. Andy thinks you're definitely good enough, and he brought it up to me earlier in the day," I replied. "It's something to think on."

"Okay, I'll give it some thought. These local events keep me kinda busy. But I imagine I can find time to do some recording," he said.

"If nothing else, maybe we can find someone with a home-based studio that will record your CDs for you. Then we can distribute them to the local radio station and those in the surrounding area," I suggested.

Humphry gave me one of those wonderful, heart-grabbing smiles.

"It sounds good to me," he told me as his eyes twinkled

I started to leave the barn, then a thought hit me, "What do you hear of your friends Tony Matthews and Rory Peters?"

The smile left his face and he replied, "Not much. They both began shunning me when the judge began booking singing engagements for me. It's like they think I don't belong in their set anymore. I think Tony has signed up for the steer roping at the upcoming rodeo. But I don't know about Rory."

HUMPHRY DID IT!

"Well, son, you're signed up for the steer roping in this upcoming rodeo too. So maybe the two of you can get together again during that time," I commented.

I left the barn thinking that it would be good for Humphry if he could connect with Tony again. After all, they had known each other, and Rory too, since the first grade. And now all three of them were starting into their junior year of high school.

Humphry had been working some with a young palomino gelding he called Mr. Gold. He had it saddle broken already. He just needed to train it. I had a sneaking suspicion Mr. Gold was his horse of choice for the steer-roping event coming up. As I thought about that, I felt a bit of excitement run through me. This gelding was the first horse Humphry had completely broken by himself, and he still had time to train it for the steer-roping event. I was proud of him. If he won the event, I could proudly claim, "Humphry did it!" all by himself.

I talked to Mr. Rayes about using a couple ranch steers for Humphry to practice on until Mr. Gold was ready. Mr. Rayes agreed to let him use them, so I suggested he tell Humphry he could use them.

"I will," he said. "And I'll also have him learn how to heel the calves for team roping. He may want to get into to that in the near future."

"Good idea," I remarked. "How would you feel about him recording some of his songs to CDs and getting them distributed to the local and surrounding radio stations?"

Mr. Rayes gave me a startled look, thought a few minutes, and then smiled and said, "I think that's a great idea! I'll check around and see if we can come up with someone who can help him record his songs. Here in Miami, the public country station is KGLC, but there are several others within driving distance of Miami."

"Thanks, Mr. Rayes," I said. "Once the CDs are recorded, he may even be able to sell a few copies at church, and maybe some of the local stores will carry them for him too."

Mr. Rayes agreed with me, telling me, "We'll see what we can do. And he's going on the ranch payroll on his birthday too. I may have to pay him cash for a couple of years, but he's a good hand, and he needs to be paid for his work."

That was something I hadn't expected. I wasn't going to tell Humphry. I would let the boss tell him on his coming birthday. I had set him up a bank account last year right after his sixteenth birthday and had been giving partial pay out of my wages. I would stop that when he was on payroll receiving his own wages.

I had set up a college fund for him right after I had finished paying Dad for the pickup.

Mr. Rayes called all us together the next morning. We had no idea what the meeting was about. We must have had question marks written all over our faces because Mr. Rayes laughed at us before telling us we were going to get some timber and build an arena out past the garden area so Humphry would have a place to practice for the rodeo events. I figured there would be some opposition, but there wasn't.

The men nodded, looked at each other, and then Bob stated, "Let's get started!"

End of conversation. We started work on the new arena. To each man, they thought of Humphry as theirs. They had all had a part in raising him. And they were as proud of him as I was. If young Humphry wanted something, they'd see that he got it with their full support.

Mr. Rayes got ahold of the manager of the KGLC radio station and talked to him about finding someone to record Humphry's CDs. The station manager asked Mr. Rayes if he could bring Humphry to the station Saturday afternoon, around three o'clock. He wanted to meet Humphry. Mr. Rayes told him he would bring Humphry and have me tag along too.

By Saturday, we had the arena finished, so Mr. Rayes gave the hired hands the day off. He had me accompany him and Humphry to the radio station where we met Ken Withers, the station manager.

When he introduced Humphry to Mr. Withers, the station manager shook his hand and, in a kindly voice, commented, "So you're the young singer I have heard about now and then."

Humphry nodded and produced a smile.

"Do you know of someone we can get to record my songs for me?" Humphry asked him.

"Follow me into this room," Mr. Withers said as he began walking to a door on his left.

He led us through the door into a room set up with several microphones, stools, recording devices, and a mixer board. I think we said in unison, "Wow!" I had never been in a recording studio, and neither had Humphry. It is probably safe to say that neither had Mr. Rayes.

Mr. Withers chuckled. He told Humphry he wanted him to play and sing one of his songs for him. Humphry hadn't brought his guitar with him as none of us expected this. Mr. Withers produced one for him to use and told him which microphone he wanted Humphry to use, then went himself to the mixer control board.

Humphry was unfamiliar with the guitar and took a few moments to check its tuning, after which he stepped to the designated microphone and began to play and sing. He seemed as much at home there as he had been at church and other local events. Mr. Rayes and I stood back out of the way and listened.

When Humphry had finished the song, Mr. Withers played it back to us as he had recorded it with the mixer board. I know I had tears brimming in my eyes. What Mr. Withers had done with Humphry's song was a miracle, I thought. It was more beautiful than I had ever dreamed possible. I was awestruck that I was listening to my son.

Mr. Withers complimented Humphry on it and told him to come back next Saturday again and he would help him create a CD that Humphry, the station, and the public listeners would be proud of. And Mr. Withers said, he would get it out to other broadcast stations. He liked Humphry's voice and his style of playing music and would help him advance his music any way he could.

31

Humphry worked with Mr. Gold in the arena, getting him used to quick breaks and speed out of the gates for the calves. And with Mr. Rayes's coaching, Hum also learned to heel the calves.

The palomino gelding proved to be a fast learner and quick on his feet and even a good cutting horse, which pleased both of them. I knew this horse was a keeper. I was proud Humphry had taught him everything he needed to know. Not only had he trained the palomino, but while he was spending time with Mom and Dad, he also did some training with Gunner; and now Gunner, even though he was getting a few years on him, was every bit as good as Mr. Gold.

He still rode his little mare, Lady, sometimes. But he had never trained her for anything but pleasure riding. From time to time, when the work was lax at the ranch, he saddled her and took her out for an afternoon leisurely ride around the vastness of the Slant T ranch.

In the evenings, he sorted out the songs he wanted to record and practiced them. Saturday promised to be a big day for him. Lyle asked to come with us. Both he and Humphry brought their own guitars with them.

Ken Withers met us at the studio door. I introduced him to Lyle and explained that it was Lyle who had taught Humphry to play.

Ken Withers smiled, shook hands, and asked, "Would you like to accompany Humphry on some of his songs? We're goin' to try to record a CD today."

"Yes, if it's okay," Lyle told him.

Ken Withers found a microphone and a stool for Lyle, in case he wanted to use it.

HUMPHRY DID IT!

"Could you play the song I did last week for Uncle Lyle?" Humphry asked.

"That's a good idea," Withers said. "Let me play that for you, and we will record the rest following that one."

Lyle listened with a smile for his student and pride in his heart for his "nephew." Me and Mr. Rayes stood back out of the way while the performance under Mr. Withers's skillful mastery of the mixer board became a full-blown CD. We all enjoyed the playback Mr. Withers had captured. It was an awesome CD. Lyle had joined in with his guitar on only four of the songs. The rest had been solely done by Humphry.

Afterward, Mr. Withers told us to wait a few minutes and he would send some copies of it home with us. We waited. It took only a few minutes for Mr. Withers to hand us CDs, complete with CD cover, song listings, and plastic cases. He gave us ten to take home and promised to make more for us if we wanted them.

"Can you make about thirty for me to take to the rodeo this Thursday and Friday afternoons? Maybe I could sell a few of them," Humphry asked.

Mr. Withers twinkled and smiled and said, "They'll be ready, Humphry, for you to pick up. And I may even bring some extra copies in case you run out."

On the way home, Lyle praised Humphry for his performance. And back at the ranch, he was the first one to tell the rest they had to come listen to the CD.

Mrs. Rayes was there to hug first Humphry and then Lyle and tell them she was proud of them. She listened as intently as everyone else when her husband put the new CD in the machine, sending the songs into the room. Afterward, the hands told Humphry and Lyle how beautiful the songs were. Each of them were given one of the CDs that had been sent home with Humphry.

"Grandma Rayes," Humphry said, "Mr. Withers is making thirty CDs for me to take to the rodeo this coming Thursday and Friday, and he said he might bring more in case I run out."

"That's wonderful, Humphry!" she exclaimed excitedly.

"Mr. Withers is also sending copies to other radio stations, and I think I can get a few people at church to buy some of them. And maybe I can get some of the local businesses to display them too. After the rodeo this week, maybe I can take some out to Grandma and Grandpa Cotton and see about getting some of the local stations out there to play it too," he told her.

"My little Humphry," she laughed, "is going to be a star one day!"

She hugged him to her.

He returned her hug and commented, "Maybe not a star, Grandma, but I enjoy making the CDs—even if it's only for my family."

"It won't be long until the whole world will be your family, Humphry. You only have two more years of high school, and with Mr. Withers helping you, who knows how far you'll be able to go with your music?" she replied.

He laughed and told her he needed to go work with Mr. Gold for a while and he still needed to brush Lady out too.

He caught the palomino gelding and saddled him and walked him to the arena. Bob and Andy hazed two young steers into the arena and into the pens at the end. Humphry rode the gelding around the arena twice before lining him up next to the first pen. He shook out his rope and nodded to Bob, who opened the gate and let the calf out. And as soon as Andy told him "go," the gelding was out and running toward the calf.

Seconds later, Humphry had the calf roped and tied, and the gelding was holding the rope taut for him. He let the calf go and put Mr. Gold on the side next to the second pen. The exercise was repeated, and the second calf was caught in record time. He let it go and rode back to the pens. Andy suggested that they do some team roping. So they hazed the calves back into the pens, which took a little effort as the calves were not wanting another workout with the horse.

"I'll catch the heads. You catch the heels," Andy told Humphry.

Andy's chestnut moved fluidly, and his roping skills were just as good. Humphry missed the first two tries at roping the heels, but eventually, he did get the calf caught by its heels. The attempts with the second calf went smoother. Humphry still needed quite a bit of practice with heeling. But Bob and Andy both told him he'd done pretty good for his first attempts.

Bob suggested they work on the team roping every day until the rodeo started. That gave them four days to practice. Humphry agreed. The calf roping and the team roping were the two things he was interested in as far as the rodeo went. He wanted to do well in both—win them if he could. So he paid attention and gave every chance his best effort. By the end of the day, he was roping heads and heels with practiced accuracy. And Mr. Gold was doing his best to be on top of it all after a few tries and figuring out what Humphry wanted him to do.

* * * * *

By Thursday afternoon, the first day of the Junior Rodeo, Humphry felt he and the gelding were both ready for either event. He registered for both. He knew several of the other contestants and made it a point to speak to them and casually told them he had recorded a CD the previous Saturday and had copies of it with him if they'd care to get one of them after the rodeo.

Tony Matthews had walked up and stood listening as Humphry relayed the information about his new CD to the other young men he was talking to.

He put a hand on Humphry's shoulder and told him, "You'd better have one of those CDs with my name on it, Hum!"

Humphry laughed and told his friend, "I'm sure I do. And I'm going to beat you at the calf roping too."

Tony smiled and said, "Wanna bet?"

Some of the others joined in the friendly cajoling about who was going to beat who in the events that were fixing to start any minute soon.

There was a large crowd this year, and Humphry was called on to sing "The Star-Spangled Banner" to open the events. He did it with zest and did it beautifully. I don't think there was a sound of any kind as his young voice sang the song. They listened. They applauded. And when they quieted down, the announcer triumphantly announced his new CD to the crowd, and he encouraged them to buy a copy of it after the rodeo on their way back to their vehicles. Humphry received another round of applause.

The second day of the Junior Rodeo, the crowd was just as large as the first day. And again Humphry was called on to sing "The Star-Spangled Banner." Again they listened quietly, and again they applauded. Once more, the announcer spoke of Humphry's new CD, encouraging those who hadn't bought one the day before to do so today on their way out of the gate to the parking lot. The crowd cheered, and Ken Withers hoped he had brought enough copies of Humphry Cotton's CD to accommodate the customers this evening.

The end totals of the calf roping put Humphry in second place by a one-second loss to Lester McGee, and Tony Matthews was two seconds behind Humphry. However, he and Tony had teamed together for the team roping event both days and became the winning team—only by a few seconds, but still a winning team.

Tony's smiling question was, "Well, what are best friends for?"

Neither of them had seen Rory Peters nor could they find anyone who had seen him. Their other friend had seemingly dropped out of sight. Tony and Humphry agreed to keep in touch with each other, no matter what.

Ken Withers had sold 1,837 of Humphry's CDs at five dollars each during the two nights of the Junior Rodeo for a total of $9,185, which he intended to give to Humphry.

But the boy would only take half of it, telling Ken Withers, "You did the work. I just sang the songs. So half of this belongs to you."

I was proud of him. I had no idea what Ken Withers had tied up in expenses producing Hum's CD and the copies he had sold at the rodeo. But I knew when Ken Withers thanked him and shook his hand that Humphry Cotton had made another friend for life. And here again I could truthfully say "Humphry did it!", because he had done it.

The Miami newspaper published a really good coverage of the Junior Rodeo and included a paragraph about Humphry's new CD and where to order them at the KGLC radio station.

I bought a copy and sent it to Mom and Dad with a copy of Hum's CD wrapped inside and asked them about bringing some of his CDs out there with us. I was sure they wouldn't mind.

HUMPHRY DID IT!

Humphry signed the front of his CD for his grandma and grandpa Cotton. He wrote them a short letter too and inserted it into the newspaper. I wished I could have been there to see their faces when they opened that package.

32

Ten days from the day I had mailed Mom and Dad the package with the newspaper, Humphry's CD, and both our letters, Humphry received a letter from Mom, praising his CD and asking him to bring extra copies with him when he came to visit so they could deliver them to the radio stations in their area and also for the church congregation to buy. She told him she and Granddad Cotton were both proud of him, and they loved him very much.

That did a lot to boost Humphry's self-confidence and self-esteem, but it didn't seem to make an imprint on his personal performances, either around the ranch or his singing engagements. He never failed to include Uncle Lyle when he played and sang locally, but both knew Uncle Lyle couldn't go to Guymon with him. There, he would be strictly on his own when singing his engagements.

Before we went to Guymon, Humphry asked Ken Withers if he would run a box of three hundred of his CDs to sell while visiting Grandma and Grandpa Cotton in Guymon. Ken, who still played and sold copies of Humphry's CDs at the station, complied.

When we picked them up, he told Humphry, "I guess you know when you get back, I'll expect you to be ready to record another cd."

He was smiling when he said it.

Humphry smiled and told him, "All right. I guess you want me to work while I'm gone."

As we neared Buffalo, I asked Humphry if it would be all right to stop at the courthouse and leave Judge Launders a copy of his CD. Humphry was agreeable to that. So we did.

We caught Judge Launders coming out of the courthouse intending to go to lunch. I spoke to him, and he stopped and looked at us questioningly.

"I'm James Cotton, and this is the youngster I brought by several years ago that you gave me custody of. I later was allowed to adopt Humphry. He's grown up to be a fine young man and has recently started recording his songs on CDs. We thought you might like to have a copy of it."

The judge smiled at Humphry, thanked him for the CD, and commented, "My Lord, James, he's almost as tall as you are. I wouldn't have recognized him."

"It's been a while. If you like the CD, you might let folks know they can order a copy of it from radio station KGLC in Miami, Oklahoma. He will be making another one in a few weeks," I told him.

Judge Launders shook hands with Humphry. "I'm proud you turned out so well, young man, and I'll do everything I can to help get your CDs sold for you. It's good to see both of you again," he said then he needed to get some lunch because he had to be back in court in just under forty-five minutes.

We needed to be back on the road again ourselves. I needed to get us routed toward Guymon, and then we needed to find a place to eat too.

"That Judge seemed awful nice," Humphry commented.

"Yes, Humphry, he can be nice and quite personable at times. In years past, though, he had a reputation for being what they call a 'hanging judge.' And I have an idea there are still those in these parts that still call him that," I told him.

"I've heard that said about Judge Holmstead too," Humphry replied. "How do they get such reputations?"

"I don't know, son. I expect it comes from not bending the law for some of those who tend to think they are above the law and that it doesn't apply to them," I said.

We stopped at a small café in Forgan and ate a hearty dinner. We could have probably gone on to Guymon, but I didn't see any sense in us piling in on Mom and Dad like a pair of starving scavengers. This café was used to feeding hungry farmers and ranchers and probably an occasional trucker too. The food was served on platters that could have used some sideboards.

Their iced tea was excellent; their lemon meringue pie was homemade, and as the expression goes—it was to die for! If anyone left this little café hungry, it was their fault.

"We'll have to remember this place," I said.

Humphry seconded the notion with an avid "Amen!"

We reached Dad's ranch roughly an hour before sundown. He and Mom both came out to give us hugs and warm welcomes.

Mom apologized for not having supper ready. I told her we had eaten already at a little café in Forgan on the way through and gave her the details of its location.

She looked thoughtful for a couple of minutes before telling me, "James, I don't recall Forgan having a café there. It must be a new one."

"New or not, Mom, they have excellent food there, and they feed their customers as if they were starved when they came through the door," I told her. "Next time you and Dad go through Forgan, you'll have to stop and check it out."

Humphry busied himself putting our things in the back bedroom where we slept when we were here. He came back to the living room now, and Dad told him how much he enjoyed the CD Humphry had sent them and also reading about how well he had done in the Junior Rodeo.

"Lamar Holmes owns the radio station here in Guymon. If you would like, we can go visit him tomorrow and take some CDs for him to play and send out to the other stations around here," Dad said to Humphry.

Humphry agreed.

"And," Dad went on, "we can stop by the livestock auction, and I can introduce you to folks I know out there too. We can take along a few of your CDs and hope you don't run out of them."

Humphry's eyes were twinkling at his Granddad Cotton's enthusiasm.

"I only brought three hundred with me, Grandpa," he told Dad. "Maybe that will be enough. When I get back, I'll be recording a second CD. They can write to the radio station in Miami and order copies of it."

Dad smiled and muttered, "My grandson, Humphry Cotton, all-around country singing star! One of these days, you'll be so popular, we'll have to buy tickets just to sneak in the back door!"

They walked down to the corral and called Gunner. He came at a lope, as eager to see Humphry as Humphry was to see him. He snickered as he came to the corral fence.

Humphry smiled and exclaimed, "Hi, Gunner old boy! I love you too."

* * * * *

After breakfast the next morning, Dad had Humphry bring twenty of his CDs along with us as we piled into his pickup and headed for Guymon. The country music station there was KGYN-AM, ran by Max Borden. Borden had been there a number of years and was one of the people who knew Dad.

He welcomed us heartily and asked Dad what brought us to his country music castle. Dad shook hands then introduced him to Humphry.

"This is my grandson Humphry Cotton. He has just recorded his first CD, which hopefully will be followed by many more once he gets out of high school. We brought a few with us. I wondered if you would listen to it."

"I'm pleased to meet you, young man. Come on in to the studio where I can listen to your CD," he invited.

The rest of us followed as he led the way. He showed us where we could sit, and then asked Humphry, "Who recorded this for you?"

Humphry told him, adding that people could also order copies of it from Ken Withers at the KGLC radio station in Miami. Max Borden smiled at him.

"Let's listen to it first and go from there," he said.

We listened, enjoying all over again the beauty of my son's voice and the music he and Lyle had put to his lyrics.

Mom had tears brimming in her eyes as she said, "That's beautiful, Humphry!"

"Yes it is," Max Borden said.

"Would you mind too much to play it on the air here at your station?" Humphry asked him.

"I'll go you one better," Borden replied. "Not only will I play it, but with your permission on a signed document, I'll see what I can do about getting it into the eyes and ears of BMI and some of the other top broadcast stations. How does that sound to you?"

Humphry lit up. His whole body seemed to shine with excitement. His face took on one of his best wonderful smiles.

He shook hands with Max Borden and answered, "That sounds great! Thank you, Mr. Borden!"

I reminded Mr. Borden that Humphry still had two more years of high school to complete.

He looked at me and said, "I'm aware of that, but he still has a summer in between those two years. That will give both of us time to work on getting him set up nationally with the public."

"I'll have to talk to my boss about letting Lyle come out with us to record the CDs or either record them first with Ken Withers and bring them with us," I told him.

Max Borden took a few minutes to think about the situation. At length, he said, "I think we can work up some suitable compromise with Ken Withers. Do you have an actual recording contract with him?"

"No, sir. But he did tell me he wants me to record another CD when I get back so that he can get it out before school starts," Humphry answered him.

"Go ahead and record that one then. Meanwhile, I will contact him and see what we can work out to get you on the road to national fame. We don't need your CDs sitting on a shelf somewhere collecting dust. But I must caution you that national popularity sometimes only lasts on average of two to three years before it starts falling off. But that's plenty of time to get you in the top ten listing," he told Humphry.

"Thank you, sir," Humphry said.

"I'm proud I met you, Humphry Cotton. I am proud to be given the opportunity to help promote your music," Borden told him. "Come into my office, and we'll get your signature on that document of permission and I'll see if I can work as hard as you have on your music."

We left the station shortly after that, a proud family following in the steps of a talented young man who was now beginning on a long life of national popularity. I had a notion that his music had been his refuge from his early life, a life he had never dwelled on since I found him alone that day at his mother's farm and took steps to adopt him. I have never regretted adopting him. I have never forgotten the first time he told his mother, "He's not a stranger. He's James, and he's my friend."

I tried to be a good dad as well as a good friend. He has grown into a fine young man of whom everyone has become proud, and the whole of the Slant T ranch consider him their family. I knew with the help of the two radio station associates, he would do well will with his music.

And he did.

He now plays an electric guitar and has become an accomplished guitarist. Somewhere along the way, he picked up a band that was as easygoing and laid back as himself. Stewart Mannor is an accomplished steel guitarist. Daniel Pherrin knows the drums inside out. And Cherry Sutton can make a fiddle do everything but dance. There again, he made all of us proud he's part of our family.

I can honestly and proudly brag that with his music—"Humphry did it!"

About the Author

Janice N. Chapman was born December 25, 1941, in Woodward, Oklahoma. She was raised on a farm south and west of Laverne, Oklahoma, and graduated high school, May 12, 1959. She began writing poetry at an early age, and through her poetic career, she received many awards, with one being the National Authors Registry in 1999, with a Presidential Recognition of Literary Excellence.

She was inducted into the International Poetry Hall of Fame October 1, 1996, and was included in the *International Who's Who in Poetry and Poets Encylopaedia* in Cambridge, England, in 1999. She was awarded the Most Admired Woman of the Decade in 1997 and also International Woman of the Year 1997–1998 and was nominated for the Professional Who's Who in 2021.

She currently lives in Harper, Kansas.

www.ingramcontent.com/pod-product-compliance
Lightning Source LLC
LaVergne TN
LVHW040058080526
838202LV00045B/3703